The World's GREATEST CRANKS AND CRACKPOTS

The World's
GREATEST CRANKS AND CRACKPOTS

Margaret Nicholas

Acknowledgements

The author wishes to thank her husband Dan for his patience and encouragement and Vic Mayhew for his enthusiasm for the original idea.

The publishers would like to thank the following organizations for their kind permission to reproduce the photographs in this book:
BBC Hulton Picture Library 33, 47, 53, 73, 83, 87, 107, 124, 152, 156, 163, 165, 168; Daily Telegraph Colour Library (M. Goddard) 113; Mary Evans Picture Library 13, 19, 22, 37, 49, 63, 97, 101, 117, 134, 136, 177, 187, 188; John Topham Picture Library 69, 92, 129, 131, 144.

First published in hardback in 1982
by Octopus Books Limited
59 Grosvenor Street
London W1

Paperback edition first published in 1984

© Octopus Books Limited

ISBN 0 7064 2149 3

Made and printed in Great Britain by
Richard Clay (The Chaucer Press) Limited
Bungay, Suffolk

Contents

Introduction

Extraordinary characters who seem unable to conform have never been more important to us than in this age of organization, planning and form-filling.

Gathered together in this book is a rich gallery of some of the most astonishing crackpots the world has ever known. It includes scores of gloriously funny stories, touching delusions and tales of bizarre adventures and adventurers.

Chapter One

STRANGE SCIENTISTS

Throughout the ages scientists have been presented as
slightly dotty characters – unkempt hair, wild-eyed
and immersed in weird theories. Some of the most
eccentric have had gloriously preposterous ideas . . .
like the man who was convinced that the world was
hollow with holes at either end . . . and the naturalist
who feasted on squirrels and earwigs . . .

Naturalist with a difference

He served his guests mice on buttered toast

'Cooked a viper for luncheon', surgeon and naturalist Frank Buckland gleefully recorded in his diary. He added that he had also prepared some elephant's trunk soup. Disappointingly, in spite of boiling for several days, the trunk itself proved too tough for eating.

Friends who called one day found him making a huge savoury pie, filled with chunks of rhinoceros. He had to admit it tasted like very ancient, very strong beef.

Lunch with Buckland, gourmet extraordinary and author of the 19th-century best-selling *Curiosities of Natural History*, was an experience of a lifetime. With his ever-inquisitive palate and incredibly strong stomach, he would sample and eat almost anything.

London Zoo provided him with some rare opportunities. Hearing that a prize panther had died he begged the curator to dig it up and send him some panther chops which, he confessed later, 'were not very good'; and after a fire at the giraffe house he was cock-a-hoop at the prospect of several weeks' supply of succulent roast giraffe.

Buckland's Regency house, on a site near Euston Station now occupied by part of the Royal College of Physicians, was a happy chaotic place, not so much a home as a menagerie. By the fire lived his monkeys. They did terrible damage and bit everyone in sight, but he loved them dearly, giving them beer every night and a drop of port on Sundays. A pet mongoose had the run of the house, pet rats scuttled over his desk and a jackass let out a wild laugh every half hour.

Buckland would stand in the middle of it all, good-humouredly puffing a cigar. Short and powerfully built, he was usually found during working hours wearing an old flannel shirt, trousers hitched under the armpits by short braces, and a bowler hat. Hating boots or shoes, he was normally barefooted.

He obviously inherited his strange culinary tastes from his father, Dr William Buckland, Dean of Westminster and one of the founders of modern geology. Buckland senior was said to have sampled a portion of Louis XIV's embalmed heart. He reckoned that the worst thing he had ever tasted was a mole but on reflection confessed to an even more unappetizing dish – stewed bluebottles. Frank's own pet aversion was earwigs. He complained they tasted terribly bitter.

Frank Buckland was born on December 17, 1826 and spent the first 20 years of his life in a splendid house on the great quadrangle of Christ Church, Oxford, where his father was then canon.

There was never a dull moment. The house was full of live creatures, most of them running free. Stuffed animals stood in the hall next to young Frank's rocking horse; snakes and green frogs were kept in cases in the dining-room.

Visitors had to be prepared to eat some strange dishes. Alligator was a rare treat for the Buckland household, mice were frequently served on buttered toast, and the famous anatomist Richard Owen and his wife were regaled with roast ostrich.

At two-and-a-half the precocious young Frank was taken to Windsor Great Park, and was not a bit frightened when he was bowled over by the kangaroos he was chasing.

When he was four his mother gave him a small natural history cabinet which he used throughout his life. He took it with him when he later left home for Winchester, the famous public school. There he would catch, dissect or stuff small animals, sometimes relieving his hunger with delicacies such as squirrel pie or mice in batter. Live pets included an owl, a buzzard, a raccoon, some jackdaws and an evil-looking magpie.

When he went on to Oxford he shared his rooms with snakes, guinea pigs, mice, frogs, a monkey, a dove and a chameleon. His pockets were always stuffed with damp moss for his slow-worms, which had a habit of poking their heads out while he was deep in conversation.

The small courtyard between his rooms and the canon's garden was turned into a miniature zoo, its inhabitants including a baby bear called 'Tig', a monkey, a jackal and an eagle. Authority would seem to have turned a blind eye until one day the eagle decided to attend eight o'clock service.

The cloister door had been left open and the huge bird found its way into the church as the Te Deum was being sung. The Dean stood petrified as Buckland's bird advanced with menacing cries. It was seized in the nick of time but apparently the Dean looked 'unspeakable things' in Buckland's direction and dealt with him later.

Deciding to become a surgeon, Frank Buckland enrolled as a student at St George's Hospital, London, in 1847. It was a time when antiseptics were unknown, when surgeons operated in any old clothes and carried whipcord for tying arteries. The suffering was appalling, but it brought out the best in Buckland. His kindness and humour made him a great favourite, especially among the poorer patients.

When his father was made Dean of Westminster, Frank returned home to live with his parents. The deanery, chaotic as ever, was a lively centre of scientific and cultural society. One day Queen Victoria's oculist, Mr White Cooper, came to dinner. After the port Frank invited him down to the cellar to inspect his pet rats. One large black specimen went straight for the reluctant visitor's ankles. 'Look out. He bites!' yelled Buckland, throwing a bag over it. In spite of his distaste, Cooper was impressed by his host's knowledge and the amusing way in which he described his pets' habits and peculiarities. He urged Buckland to put the information down on paper and promised to find a publisher. Buckland's fascinating article on rats eventually appeared in a magazine called *Bentley's Miscellany*, and proved a landmark. Nobody had written like this about animals, particularly rodents. It was the first of a series later published as *Curiosities of Natural History*.

Though commissioned as an assistant surgeon in the Life Guards, he devoted more and more of his time to natural history, being much in demand as a writer and lecturer. He also became involved in one of the most eccentric schemes ever devised in Victorian England, becoming a founder member of the Society for the Acclimatization of Animals in the United Kingdom.

A rapidly rising population needed new and cheaper sources of meat. Why not fill the great parks of Britain with kangaroos, yaks and bison? Once acclimatized, they would provide juicy steaks for everyone. The capybara, largest rodent in the world, was a fast breeder, but perhaps not very appetizing. Chinese sheep were actually imported at great expense from Shanghai, but for some reason failed to breed.

At the annual dinner of the Society in 1862 Buckland's menu was enormous, including kangaroo stew, wild boar and roast curassow (a tough South American bird). The company chewed its way through the gargantuan feast for two and a half hours; but not all appreciated Buckland's pièce de résistance, stewed tripang or Japanese sea-slug. 'They are said to be the most succulent and pleasant food, not unlike the green fat of turtle,' wrote Buckland in gleeful anticipation. In the event even he had to admit they tasted like something between calf's head jelly and the contents of a glue pot.

Buckland's home life was very happy. His house became well known for its peculiar assortment of visitors. Children would climb the railings to gawp at the giants and dwarfs, circus freaks and fairground folk who were asked to tea along with scientists and politicians. He was very fond of the famous Siamese twins, Chang and Eng.

His wife Hannah shared his love of animals, often caring for small, sick zoo animals. One patient was a very tiny, very rare South African red river hog. She managed to rear it but as it grew it became increasingly boisterous. Its favourite trick was to crawl under a dining-room chair during dinner and raid the table at the first opportunity. As it grew larger it often became firmly

Frank Buckland

wedged. One night a solemn clergyman found himself travelling steadily backwards from the table towards the door. He was furious at the indignity. Clearly the red river hog had to go!

In 1861 Buckland hatched his first perch and began a new career that was to occupy him for the rest of his life – fish farming. He set up a hatchery in his Albany Street home and joked that as he had hatched 30,000 salmon in his kitchen and since that noble fish always returned to his birthplace, one day there was obviously going to be a problem!

Much of his own money was spent setting up a museum of fish culture in South Kensington. Queen Victoria went to see it and was so impressed she invited him to pay a visit to her home at Frogmore.

In 1867, to his delight, he was appointed Inspector of H.M. Salmon Fisheries. This took him up and down the country to look into the state of rivers and make sure that the salmon could negotiate weirs and other man-made obstacles on their way to the sea. Where necessary, he set up salmon 'ladders' to help them. At one particularly difficult spot he left them a notice: 'No road at present over this weir. Go downstream, take the first turn to the right and you will find good travelling water upstream and no jumping required. F.T.B.'

His stocky, bearded figure became well known on the railways, but because his fishy luggage smelt so awful he was usually given a carriage to himself.

He cared little for personal comfort. Year after year he waded through icy rivers, testing the force of the current with his chest, building his ladders and catching fish eggs for hatcheries. In winter he would rub himself all over with hair oil and wear a waterproof suit, which as often as not froze solid and clung to him like a suit of armour.

In January 1878 the New Zealand government sent an urgent request for an extra shipment of salmon ova. It was too late in the season for 'ripe' fish, but Buckland went from river to river, sometimes standing for hours in the freezing water, hardly able to see for the driving snow. He caught the steamer in time but the effort proved too much even for his burly frame. As a result of asthma and inflammation of the lungs he had to abandon all outdoor work. When dropsy set in and surgeons wanted to operate, he refused chloroform on the grounds that he wanted to see the operation.

Frank Buckland was only 54 when he died on December 19, 1880. He anticipated his death with characteristic good humour. In his will he wrote: 'God is so good, so very good to little fishes. I do not believe he would let their inspector suffer shipwreck at last. I am going on a long journey where I think I shall see a great many curious animals ... this journey I must go alone.'

The complete traveller

He discovered fingerprints and dreamed up a master race

Should you feel under the weather when travelling in remote foreign parts, just drop a charge of gunpowder into a tumbler of warm, soapy water and toss it down. That was the advice of Francis Galton in a little gem of a book called *The Art of Travel*. It will tickle the throat, he admitted, but clear the system.

Sore feet? Blisters? Simply make a lather of soap suds inside your socks and break a raw egg into each boot to soften the leather. Lice could be dealt with by taking half an ounce of mercury, mixing it with old tea leaves and spit, and making a little necklace of beads to hang round the neck.

Wasp stings? Well, the goo scraped out of a tobacco pipe and smeared on the skin works as well as anything. And should you be plagued by scurvy, treacle and lime juice spread on the gums will stop your teeth falling out.

Galton's book proved a best-seller and ran to five editions. It covered every contingency, from constructing boats, huts and tents in a hurry to sending up distress signals in the bush or catching fish without a line. It told readers how to find firewood in a rainstorm (under the roots of a tree), how to deal with the locals (a frank, joking but determined manner is best) and how to keep your clothes dry when it pours (just take them off and sit on them).

The horse, he found, was a very useful animal to have around when travelling. It could always be used as a wind-shield, and if you wanted to light your pipe in a hurricane all you had to do was to creep under its belly and stay there. If you wanted to cross a river and the horse was a reluctant swimmer, the best solution, said Galton, was to lead it along a steep bank and, when its mind was on other things, take it by surprise and shove it in sideways.

He offered his encyclopaedic knowledge of survival to the War Office when, at the outbreak of the Crimean War in 1855, it was demonstrated how helpless the average British soldier was when faced with primitive conditions. He was invited to give lectures at the newly-founded Army camp at Aldershot, but only a few turned up to hear him. The hard-headed military considered him a crank.

Yet Francis Galton was a remarkable man. He is probably best remembered as one of the first men to discover that every human being has a different set of fingerprints. His method of classifying them is still used in criminal investigation. He also invented the word association test and wrote a book on heredity that changed the ideas of a generation. But it is his genius for solving life's everyday problems that makes him endearing. Nothing was too humdrum to escape his attention.

He came from a family of Quakers and businessmen, many of whom took a keen interest in science. His grandfather, Samuel, made a fortune by manufacturing guns (to the dismay of his co-religionists) and founded the Galton bank in Birmingham. This was inherited by Galton's father, Samuel Tertius, who found it a burden and would much rather have devoted his life to scientific study. Through his mother, he was related to Charles Darwin, the great naturalist.

Francis Galton was born on February 16, 1822 in a handsome Georgian mansion, littered with microscopes and telescopes, called The Larches which stood, surrounded by fields, in the Sparkbrook district of Birmingham. He was the last of seven children and enjoyed a happy childhood.

When he was 16 he decided to become a doctor and was accepted for training at Birmingham General Hospital. In the dispensary, he discovered the Pharmacopoeia, which listed all the medicines in current use. He felt he would never be satisfied until he knew, from personal experience, the effect they all had on the human system.

Starting with those listed under the letter A, he began to work his way through the alphabet. Nothing drastic seems to have happened until he came nearly to the end of the letter C. Then he encountered Croton Oil, a particularly strong purgative.

'I foolishly believed that two drops of it could have no noticeable effect,' he wrote in his memoirs, 'But indeed they had. I can recall them now ....' When he recovered he decided to abandon the investigation and went on to bandaging and splints.

When Galton took his degree, however, at Trinity College, Cambridge, it was not in medicine, but mathematics. He had worked so hard that he swore the effort had given him a 'sprained brain'. Concerned about the possible over-heating of his mental equipment, he invented a ventilated hat, which would let the fresh air circulate around his cranium. It had tiny shutters which worked by means of a valve, operated by a small bulb in the end of a rubber tube dangling from the crown.

He was never particularly happy as a member of the medical profession – he hated post mortems – and when his father's death left him with sufficient money to make himself independent, he decided he would rather pursue a healthier life.

Longing for the wide open spaces, he left for Syria, Egypt and the Sudan. Then, with the encouragement of the Royal Geographical Society, he travelled through the little known, vast territories of South West Africa.

As an explorer he was in the great Victorian tradition, enduring both hardship and danger to break new ground. But true to his nature, he tackled Africa in a brisk, practical, no-nonsense English manner. Furious when he heard that members of a certain Hottentot tribe were killing off missionaries, he set out to 'examine the situation' and totally demoralized their chief by riding into his kraal on a snorting ox and telling him to stop it.

On another occasion he was presented by the Chief of the Ovampo tribe with a voluptuous princess as a temporary wife. Galton turned her out of his tent, explaining huffily: 'She was covered with red ochre and butter and I was dressed in my one well preserved suit of white linen. . . .'

As a scientist he was interested in the genetic reasons which caused Hottentot women to have such enormous bottoms. One day, spotting a veritable Venus preening herself under a tree, he made up his mind to get her vital statistics. Not speaking the language and reluctant to consult a missionary, his sprained brain eventually came up with the bright idea of surveying her from a distance with his sextant. He measured her up, translated the results into trigonometry and logarithms and later wrote a solemn paper on the subject.

After two years and an arduous journey of 1,700 miles – often through territory where no white man had been before – he returned home to record his travels and to receive his accolades: the Gold Medal of the Royal Geographical Society, Fellowship of the Royal Society and membership of the Athenaeum Club. With relish, he set to work on *The Art of Travel* and sealed his success with a best-seller.

In 1853 he proposed to Louisa Butler, daughter of the Dean of Peterborough. They were to remain married for 44 years and Galton was devoted to her. But she did not make life easy for him. Louisa was something of a martinet, rather mean and a hypochondriac. She used to prepare for death at regular intervals and 'Aunt Louisa's dying again' became a common saying in the family. They never had children, which was sad for he got on well with young people. Every Christmas he would draw a number of newly minted sovereigns from the bank and press them into the palms of his numerous nephews and nieces, cautioning them in a whisper not to tell their Aunt Louisa.

In 1857 he bought a house in South Kensington, London, about a quarter of a mile from the Science Museum. From the outside, Number 42 Rutland Gate was no different from thousands of other respectable, solidly built town houses. But inside it presented a revolutionary interior for an age which almost smothered itself in antimacassars, stuffy hangings and plump velvet furniture.

Galton insisted that everything in his home must have a practical purpose, partly because he suffered from asthma, but also because of his highly individual attitude to everyday things. Carpets, curtains and wallpaper collected dust – so he refused to have them. Visitors found themselves sliding over parquet floors that shone like glass, sitting bolt upright in plain wooden chairs that offered no comfort. The house was full of his inventions, including a signal that warned people throughout the house whenever the lavatory was engaged. He explained: 'It saves a futile climb upstairs and the occupant is not subjected to the embarrassment of having the door handle rattled.'

In middle life Galton was a distinguished looking man with a fine, domed head, formidable eyebrows and piercing, quizzical grey eyes. Unfortunately, he was not very tall. This was a drawback when it came to watching processions and ceremonies, which he loved with the fervour of a small boy. As usual, he had a practical solution. He would arrive on the scene with a large wooden brick, wrapped in brown paper, tucked under his arm. Oblivious to stares, he would lower the brick to the ground with a piece of rope and stand on it. Then he would take from his pocket a gadget he had invented called a 'hyperscope' – rather like a miniature periscope – which gave him a splendid view over hats and heads. The ceremony over, he would hoist up his brick, pocket his hyperscope and hurry home to dinner.

In the natural world, meteorology interested him most and his passionate belief in statistics enabled him to prepare weather charts more accurate than any seen before. In the course of his work he discovered and named the anti-cyclone.

His principal interest, however, was the study of heredity. The publication in 1859 of his cousin Charles Darwin's book *The Origin of Species* opened his mind to new ideas and gave him the courage to pursue a line of thought that had haunted him for years – how to improve the human race. In his revolutionary work *Hereditary Genius*, he set out to prove, with a mountain of statistics, that ability and talent are inherited. This being so, he argued, more perfect human beings could only be produced by selective breeding between those who had abilities to pass on, and who were physically and mentally sound.

His blueprint for producing a master race was avidly discussed by all the learned bodies of the day and dealt with portentously in the columns of *The Times*. He coined the title 'eugenics' for his new science. It all seemed perfectly logical. From the scientific viewpoint, better strains would be created if the same care were taken over breeding human beings as over horses and livestock. This pillar of Victorian society would have been

Francis Galton in 1864

appalled had he known that one day his theories would be seized upon by the Nazis and used as an excuse to commit the most monstrous crimes in recent history.

Galton set up an 'anthropometric' laboratory at the International Health Exhibition, held at South Kensington in 1884. Here he set out to collate a vast volume of physical facts by measuring people – taking their weight, height, span, reaction time, keenness of sight, size of heads and length of stride. He also collected their thumb prints.

The public turned up in their thousands to have their statistics taken. But it was only when he had studied his 2,500 individual thumb prints that he began to realize they were all different. He transferred his laboratory to a permanent site in the South Kensington Museum, began to take prints from all ten fingers, and by 1893 had enough material to publish a 200-page book called simply *Fingerprints*, which is the basis for identification in criminal investigations to this day.

What appeals most about Galton is the contrast between the lofty nature of his mind and the delightfully barmy nature of so many of his practical experiments. He decided, for instance, to make a chart showing which part of Britain had the most beautiful girls. He invented a pocket mechanical device which recorded numbers whenever he pressed a button. Then off he went on a tour of the big cities, strolling through the busy streets, scrutinizing female passers-by and pressing his button when he came across a beauty. At the end of this exhausting survey he declared that London had the highest quota of beautiful women – and Aberdeen the lowest!

His experiments in anthropology included one which tested human and animal sensitivity to high notes. He invented what became known as the Galton whistle, which could be made to produce extremely high pitched noises around and above the human threshold. Fixed into a hollow walking stick, it could be operated by squeezing a rubber bulb under the handle. On fine days Galton would take up his stick, saunter out, find some unfortunate creature minding its own business, hold the stick close to its ear, and squeeze the bulb. If the creature nearly jumped out of its skin, he knew it had heard the note. If it ignored the whole procedure, it had not.

Of all the animals tested, cats were found to be the most sensitive and dogs the least responsive. Insects he found utterly hopeless, but he had amazing success at the zoo, where he managed to upset all the lions.

Measuring human reactions had become a passion. Friends who came to dinner at Rutland Gate might have been alarmed if they had known what was going on. He reckoned that if two people were attracted to each other they would slope together when they sat side by side. If indifferent or cool, they would sit bolt upright. He fitted pressure drums to the legs of his dining room chairs and when his guests had gone home examined the imprint they had left and calmly came to his own conclusions.

Galton's wife died in 1879 and from then on he never seemed to be without the company of a charming woman. Eva Biggs, the grand-daughter of his late sister, Lucy, moved into Rutland Gate with him and he described her as 'a capital companion, always cheerful and punctual and interested'.

He received many academic honours in his later years and in June 1909, at the age of 87, he was knighted. But by this time the asthma he had suffered from all his life and attacks of chronic bronchitis had weakened him considerably, and he was not fit enough to attend the investiture.

For many years he had gone abroad for the winter, but in 1910 the effort of travelling to the softer air of Italy or southern France was too much for him. Instead he took a house at Hindhead in Surrey for the cold season, hoping to regain some of his strength. When he saw the sharp turn at the top of the stairs leading to his bedroom he remarked calmly: 'This will be an awkward corner to get my coffin round.' He died peacefully in his bed only a month or so after moving in on January 17, 1911. Too weak to eat, he had smilingly refused food with a quotation from Robert Burns:

'Some hae meat and canna eat it
And some wad eat that want it.'

Francis Galton was practical to the last.

Holes at the Poles

He planned a journey to the centre of the Earth

After studying the universe, John Cleves Symmes came to the conclusion that the Earth must be hollow, with room inside for five other planets. He was quite positive, moreover, that there were gaping holes at both the North and South Poles and that it was possible to sail into them to find out what was going on inside. He confidently expected to discover another race of human beings, swarming animal life and luxurious vegetation: perhaps even the answer to the mystery of life itself.

So convincing was Symmes, and so persuasive a talker, that in January 1823 United States congressmen were prepared to listen politely to a request to finance his proposed expedition to the centre of the Earth.

Captain Symmes, an army veteran, had drawn up his plans with meticulous attention to detail. He had decided, he explained, to tackle the North hole first. For this attempt he would need 100 'brave companions', including scientists, two ships and enough reindeer and sleighs to carry his expedition over the frozen wastes of Siberia, from where he planned to set out. He would sail to the hole – which he estimated was 4,000 feet in

John Cleves Symmes

diameter – through the Bering Strait. Asked whether he expected to drop off the edge, he solemnly replied that he rather thought they would just sail on and eventually find themselves inside. They might not even know the historic moment at which they entered the bowels of the earth!

Who was this dazzling adventurer?

John Cleves Symmes was a shopkeeper, a dreamer and a bookworm. He came from an old Puritan family and was born in Sussex County, New Jersey on November 5, 1780. The only member of the Symmes clan who had done anything distinguished was an uncle who helped found the city of Cincinnati.

Young John had always been fascinated by science, exploration and the stars. Everyday life seemed very mundane to him. When he was 22 he decided on a military career, perhaps attracted by the chance of excitement and glory. His early days were spent in drab, primitive forts in the Mid-West but he once enlivened the tedium by fighting a duel in which he nearly killed his opponent and himself sustained an injury. His great moment came when he fought with the United States army in the 1812 war against Great Britain – the war that produced 'The Star Spangled Banner' – when he rose to the rank of captain and became something of a hero, leading a company with 'bravery, skill and gallantry' in a particularly bloody skirmish.

When he retired from the army in 1816 he became a trader. The government granted him a licence to sell supplies to the Indians and government troopers and he set up shop at a trading post at St Louis, out in the wilds of Missouri. It was a lonely life and to keep him company he married a war widow with six children, later adding four more of his own to the family.

Trade and domestic life didn't interest him very much, though he was pleased enough with the arrival of one son to dignify him with the name Americus Vespucius. Most of his time he had to be dragged away from some book he was reading on scientific discovery to sell canned beans and socks.

He was fascinated by outer space and bought a telescope so that he could gaze at Jupiter on clear Missouri nights. He studied charts and drawings of Saturn and concluded that the presence of rings around the planet verified the theory of concentric spheres or hollow planets.

Sitting on his stoop on hot summer nights Symmes also came to the conclusion that Sir Isaac Newton had been barking up the wrong tree and that an atmosphere 'filled with microscopically invisible hollow spheres of ether' accounted for gravity.

The idea of a hollow planet seemed more and more logical to him. After all hadn't nature made the interior of animal bones, wheat stalks and human hair completely hollow? Formless matter in rotation took the shape of spheres, so, he argued, 'a nebular mass in rotation, as our Earth during its

23

formation, would not assume the form of a solid sphere, but a hollow one. . . .'

He searched through his books to find supporting evidence and in the process brought to light some mind-blowing theories. The Babylonians, to start with, believed the world was a hollow mountain supported and surrounded by the sea. Inside this mountain lay the dark world of the dead. He read the writings of a certain Professor Burnet who believed the Earth had once been a small core covered with oil to which the fluid of the atmosphere had clung, thus forming the Earth's crust. There was another professor who said the Earth was made of distinct strata, like onion skins, and yet another convinced it was like an egg with shell, albumen and yolk.

Symmes was extremely excited when he found a German mathematician who was certain there was another planet in the centre of the Earth which had daylight and a prospering civilization. But what finally convinced him was when he realized that even Halley, the great 17th-century Astronomer Royal, who had a comet named after him, had talked about three planets spinning in a void under the Earth's crust.

Jumbling together all he had read, he was quite positive he would find *five* more planets inside the Earth, fitting into each other like parts of a Chinese puzzle. Each would have an opening filled with a very light, elastic substance, with the nature of hydrogen gas. Ocean currents would gush through these openings and he would drift through from planet to planet.

By the spring of 1818 he could contain himself no longer. The world had to know about his great theory and he would have to raise money to finance an expedition. From the trading post way out in Missouri he posted 500 pamphlets announcing his plans to people likely to wield enough influence to help him. With these notices he thoughtfully included a medical bulletin stating that he was in his right mind.

Soon, he realized, he would have to make a direct appeal to the public; so he moved his large family to Newport, Kentucky, where he might be nearer to people with money and power. He set out on a lecture tour that drew huge audiences. People sat open-mouthed with astonishment as he described with utter conviction the warm, rich lands stocked with lush vegetation and swarming with wildlife that lay waiting for the explorer. He believed a new race of humans would be discovered but did not dare guess what form they would take.

Unfortunately, he flew into the most awful tempers at the slightest sign of ridicule and resented questions that probed too deeply. But he made a terrific impression on many listeners, including Richard M. Johnson, a United States Representative who was to become Vice President of America. It was Johnson who actually asked Congress to equip and fit out two ships for Symmes. He was very disappointed when the whole project, after discussion, was passed over as 'unsound'.

This did not in the least deter Symmes. He produced all sorts of rational arguments. For instance, he said, explorers often reported that mysterious warm air currents melted ice in the polar seas: these currents obviously rose from the great cavities at the Poles.

Asked by sceptical listeners how he would be able to see without sunlight, he explained that he did not think that it would be totally dark ... there would be a soft congenial glow produced by the sun's rays as they slanted through the hole.

By 1823 Symmes was ready once more to appeal for support. He had managed to raise a petition bearing hundreds of names, including some extremely distinguished ones.

He pointed out that his expedition would not only be a wonderful opportunity for making new discoveries in geography, natural history and geology, but would also present exciting commercial possibilities. Perhaps it was the prospect of expanding trade that encouraged Johnson to press Symmes's case once more. At any rate, when a vote was taken in the House of Representatives 25 Congressmen signified their readiness to send him off to Siberia with as many reindeer, sleighs and 'brave comrades' as he required. Unfortunately, they did not form a majority, and after much wrangling and dispute over procedure the whole business was allowed to sink into oblivion.

Symmes went on with his lectures and was somewhat gratified to know that the polar openings were now officially described as 'Symmes Holes'. But the strain proved too much for him. On one of his strenuous lecture tours, in Canada, he fell ill and had to be rushed home. He died on May 29, 1829 when he was only 49 years old.

Happily, that was not the end of his brave ideas. His son, Americus Vespucius Symmes, gathered all his father's writings together in one book and established him as the originator of the 'Symmes Theory of Concentric Spheres and Polar Voids'. He firmly believed in them and added a theory of his own – that the ten lost tribes of Israel would one day be found deep in the bowels of the Earth.

Writer Jules Verne, always on the lookout for a good story, pounced on Symmes's theory with delight and used it as the basis for his *Journey to the Centre of the Earth*. One of his characters, Dr. Clawbonny, remarks: 'In recent times it has even been suggested that there are great chasms at the Poles; it is through these that there emerges the light which forms the Aurora, and you can get down through them into the interior of the Earth ...' As the plot unfolds, it becomes clear that Symmes made his historic exploration after all, even though it was only between the covers of a book!

GREAT PRETENDERS

Some people seem to be unable to live with their own characters. They long to be bigger, bolder and more colourful ... like the shaven lady who thought she was the Queen of the Jews ... and the bankrupt who proclaimed himself Emperor of America ...

Emperor Joshua of the USA

He abolished congress and levied taxes

The Emperor held court in a shabby, rented room furnished with a camp bed, a table and chair, a faded rug and a broken washstand. His regalia hung on nails knocked into the walls, and pictures of Queen Victoria and the Empress Eugénie covered damp patches on the wallpaper.

But frequent callers at the 50-cents-a-day boarding house in San Francisco bowed and curtsied as they entered. And when the Emperor thundered on about the state of the Union and his intention to abolish Congress, they listened politely.

For they were in the presence, no less, of his Imperial Highness Norton I, Emperor of the United States of America.

Joshua Abraham Norton was 40 years old and bankrupt when he decided that America was drifting towards disaster and needed to be ruled by a firm, autocratic monarch. As there seemed to be no one else in the running, he resolved to take the job himself.

One evening in September 1859, he called on the editor of the *San Francisco Bulletin* and left an impressive document proclaiming himself Emperor of the United States. So extraordinary was his bearing that the editor not only accepted it, he printed it on the front page.

For the next 21 years, Emperor Norton revelled in his self-appointed task. The astonished and amused citizens of San Francisco went along with him. He declared the abolition of Congress as he had promised, printed his own bonds, levied his own taxes and turned up uninvited at glittering diplomatic functions.

Stocky, bearded and dignified, he strode about the streets of San Francisco wearing a pale blue army officer's uniform with gold epaulettes and brass buttons, a tall black hat with a bright green plume and a pair of outsize boots slit at the sides to make room for his corns. A heavy sabre, bought from a local blacksmith, clanked at his heels.

Few people guessed that once he had been a shrewd and wealthy businessman.

Norton was born in London in February 1819 but when he was only an infant his father, John, emigrated to South Africa. He joined the pioneer farmers, bought land and helped to found what is now Port Elizabeth.

Once his farm was established, John Norton set up as a ships' chandler. He prospered further and soon owned several vessels. Joshua worked for him, first as a clerk, then as master of one of his ships sailing from Cape Town to Chile and Peru.

South America appealed to Joshua's flamboyant imagination, and when his father died, leaving him the business, he sold up and headed for Brazil.

He might have stayed there, ending his days as a solid merchant, but in 1849 news came of the fabulous gold strike in California. Joshua arrived in San Francisco carrying his 40,000-dollar savings in a trunk, determined to join the Forty-niners in the gold rush.

After a shrewd look round he realized he stood more chance of making a fortune by trading in the boom town itself than by prospecting in the gold fields. He opened an office and invested his savings.

He lived by importing coal, bricks, tea, flour and beef, holding them until they were in great demand, then selling at a huge profit. His fortune grew to 250,000 dollars. Norton invested the entire amount in rice – and in 1856 was declared bankrupt.

At this point he decided he was through with commerce. His life had been spent in fiercely competitive trade. Now it had all come to nothing. He left his elegant town house, rented a room and shut himself away to brood.

Fortunately he had one great asset – his friends. His flamboyant personality had made him well liked. Even his old business colleagues did not forget him.

They called on him only to find that he had become immersed in the troubles of America. He spoke of little else. He told them war between the North and South was inevitable unless a firm ruler took over. His visitors began jokingly to address him as 'Emperor' and 'Your Majesty'.

He took them seriously, drafted his historic proclamation and delivered it to the editor of the *Bulletin*.

Soon afterwards he appeared for the first time in court dress. There was always a rose in the buttonhole of his shabby tunic and he walked with a regal air. In good weather he flourished a walking stick and, when it rained, a garish Chinese umbrella. He was usually followed by two mongrel dogs and a horde of children.

The government, he announced, was riddled with fraud and corruption. He issued an edict: 'We do hereby abolish Congress and it is hereby abolished.' He was incensed when nobody took any notice and issued a further decree in which he dissolved the Republic. About this time, too, he declared himself 'Protector' of Mexico.

He soon realized that he could not carry on his great work without revenue. First he tried selling bonds illustrated with his own portrait. When they did not prove successful he invented a system of taxation. Regularly, in full court dress, he would call on people he knew and others he found in the trade directory. Small shopkeepers were let off with a 25-cents tax; more affluent businessmen were charged three dollars. Few people refused him. On a good day the Emperor could expect to take home about 25 dollars.

People he met in the street bowed and curtsied. He would pause to inspect drains, check public transport timetables and discuss the crime rate with local police.

He always ate out, often at fashionable restaurants, and was seldom presented with a bill. He rode free of charge on public transport and had complementary seats for the theatre.

Once he was arrested on a vagrancy charge and spent the night in a police cell. Next day the police chief rushed to his aid and offered profuse apologies. Newspapers denounced this offence against His Majesty. One editor wrote: 'He has shed no blood, robbed nobody, deprived nobody of his country, which is more than can be said for most fellows in his line.'

The greatest crisis in his reign came when his uniform started to fall to pieces. He issued another of his edicts: 'I, Norton I, have heard serious complaints from our adherents that our Imperial Wardrobe is a national disgrace ...' Men's outfitters in the city took the hint.

One of his favourite pastimes was to write to monarchs and heads of state in other countries. At the outbreak of the American Civil War in 1861, he sent letters to President Lincoln and Jefferson Davis, president of the Confederacy, ordering them to join him in San Francisco so that he could mediate. They did not reply. Undaunted, he tackled Bismarck during the Franco-Prussian War, frequently sending him advice.

He was always having ideas. Most of them were dismissed as impractical, if not crazy, but one remains as a constant memorial to him. It was Joshua Norton who first suggested that a suspension bridge should be built across San Francisco Bay. Half a century later it became a reality.

When, in 1880, Joshua Norton collapsed in a street and died, in full uniform, San Francisco went into mourning. People wept openly as they read newspaper headlines announcing: 'The King is Dead'. After 21 years they could not imagine the place without him. More than 10,000 loyal subjects filed past his rosewood coffin to pay their last respects. Joshua Norton would have been satisfied.

His was a funeral worthy of an Emperor.

'Queen' of the Jews

Lady Hester waited to wed the new Messiah

Shut away from the world in an isolated monastery in the hills of Lebanon, one of the most remarkable women of the last century waited to become Queen of the Jews.

Lady Hester Stanhope, once a glamorous figure in London society, had been told by fortune-tellers and self-styled prophets that this was to be her destiny.

The predictions had started long ago in England. They were repeated again in the East. Passages from scriptures and lines from ancient Arab manuscripts had been shown to her to prove she was to become the long-awaited bride of a new Messiah.

Transformed by years of exotic wanderings in Syria, Palestine and Lebanon, her life as an English aristocrat a thing of the past, Lady Hester began to believe the predictions.

How else could one explain her strange life?

Curious travellers from Europe called to pay their respects at the home she created for herself from the half-ruined and abandoned monastery of Mar Elias. Stories had filtered back to England of how this daughter of the great Chatham family had abandoned her life as a European and had become a legend in the Middle East.

Visitors found a statuesque, commanding woman, nearly six feet tall, dressed like a male Turk in voluminous trousers, her head shaved and covered by a turban. As her guests talked, she filled the room with smoke, puffing continually at her Turkish chibouk.

They could hardly believe that this was the niece of William Pitt the Younger, one of the greatest of British prime ministers. She had been famous as his hostess at Walmer Castle – a lady of fashion and an ornament of the London drawing rooms.

Now they discovered her absorbed by the East and obsessed with mysticism and astrology. She had power and influence among the Arabs and many of the ruling sheiks regarded her with awe. They had never met an English woman – indeed, any woman – quite like her before.

It was in 1810, when she was 33 years old, that life in England turned sour for Lady Hester. First came the death of her beloved uncle, Pitt, then that of her favourite brother, Charles. This was crowned by a bitter disappointment in love.

She decided to take a long sea voyage to revive her sad spirits. Accompanied by a small group of admirers – including her physician, Dr Charles Meryon, and a young man called Michael Bruce, who was to become her lover – she set out to forget her troubles and see the world.

She was never to return.

With her friends, time passed pleasantly enough. They reached Athens, where the poet Byron was said to have dived into the sea off Piraeus to greet her, and then went on to Constantinople. Cairo was to be their next destination.

They set sail, ran into terrible storms, and were shipwrecked off the island of Rhodes, losing all their possessions. No European clothes could be found on the island, so the whole party had to dress in Eastern costume.

Lady Hester refused to wear the veil or dress of the Eastern woman. Instead, she wore Turkish male clothes: a long robe, turban and yellow slippers. And this was how she dressed for the rest of her life.

When she eventually reached Cairo on board a British frigate which had called to rescue the shipwrecked travellers, she bought a new outfit so that she could appear before the Pasha in style.

In his memoirs, Dr Meryon said she purchased a robe of purple velvet encrusted with gold embroidery (cost unknown), two cashmere shawls at £50 each, embroidered trousers at £40, waistcoat and jacket – another £50. Her sabre cost £20 and her saddle £35. It still took another £100 to complete her outfit. She looked so impressive that when she entered his palace, the Pasha rose to greet her.

Regardless of expense, she then set out on a series of spectacular journeys through the Middle East, riding on a magnificent Egyptian saddle of crimson velvet embroidered with gold, her lavish costume covered with a white hooded cloak.

She was received with great wonder and awe by many of the sheiks who took her to be some strange English princess of fabulous wealth. Many people warned her that it would be unwise to enter a city unveiled but she ignored them. Even in Damascus, then the most fanatical of Moslem cities, where Christians were despised, she rode side-saddle with her proud profile exposed for all to see.

Some took her for a young man whose beard had not grown. But those who realized she was a woman were bemused. They did not know what to make of her. Fortunately, they were cautious and treated her with respect, pouring coffee before her horse as she rode by.

Lady Hester Stanhope's bedroom at Djoun

In Jerusalem she was formally received by the governor. When it was known that she was on her way to the church of the Holy Sepulchre, the doors were first closed in her face, then flung wide open to allow her to enter – a mark of great respect.

Increasingly, Lady Hester began to see herself as an exotic heroine with a mystical destiny. Her friends jokingly called her Queen Hester and she began to take them seriously.

Her loyal English retinue dwindled as the cost of her travelling rose, but she was still attended by the indomitable Mrs Anne Fry, who was as English as muffins and must have hated every minute of it.

The greatest journey was yet to come. Lady Hester was passionately determined to visit the ruins of the great city of Palmyra in the Arabian Desert. Until then, only three Englishmen had reached it. The route across the sands was infested with tribes of fierce Bedouin who would rob and kill without mercy.

She dressed as a Bedouin and set out with a fantastic caravan which included 22 camels and mountains of luggage. A black slave armed with an axe guarded her tent at night. Sheiks came from all parts of the desert to see this extraordinary woman 'with the courage of a lion and the eyes of an eagle'.

Her reputation preceded her. When she reached Palmyra she was received like a queen of the desert and crowned in a celebration pageant. It must have seemed as though the prophecies were coming true.

By 1814 she had had enough of wandering and found the disused monastery of Mar Elias on a hilltop overlooking the sea near Sidon in Lebanon. She created a beautiful garden there and conducted her household strictly in the Turkish manner.

From Mar Elias she wielded considerable influence over her Arab neighbours, refusing to be cowed by local rulers and offering sanctuary to refugees whenever there were religious wars. She sheltered hundreds of them over the years. Feeding them alone cost her a fortune.

When Mar Elias became too small to house her refugees and when the faithful Dr Meryon returned home at last, she moved to Djoun, another ruined monastery farther into the mountains with not even a nearby village.

From there she kept up correspondence with some of the greatest names of her day. Travellers to whom the name of Hester Stanhope had become a legend would go out of their way to visit her. Many reported that her brilliant mind was being wasted. She could keep up a conversation for eight or nine hours at a stretch, hypnotizing her listeners.

She continued to be lavishly generous, partly to maintain her importance in the eyes of the Arabs, partly because she had no money sense whatsoever.

Assuming that the British government would foot the bill, she mounted an extravagant expedition to search for buried treasure in the ancient city of Ascalon. The expedition was a flop and the British government was not even remotely interested.

Financially it was the last straw. She was deeply in debt and the pension she relied on from England was stopped to pay off her foreign creditors. She became involved in an interminable wrangle with Lord Palmerston, Queen Victoria's prime minister, who had given the order to cut off her money.

Furious, she wrote to the Queen upbraiding her for allowing Palmerston to behave in such a high-handed manner. 'There is no trifling with those who have Pitt blood in their veins', she informed Her Majesty.

As the years went by, she became more eccentric. She would not receive visitors until it was dark. Then, folding a cashmere turban over her now shaven head, she would sit so that the light fell only on her hands and face, which still retained some of their former beauty.

Her roof leaked. Her servants stole everything of value. After Palmerston's action, she sealed up all the entrances to the monastery, leaving only one door for cattle to go to and fro.

No one called her Queen Hester any more.

She died peacefully at Djoun in June 1839, at the age of 63. When the British consul from Beirut arrived at the monastery to deal with her affairs, he found that 35 rooms had been sealed up to prevent robbery.

He opened them expecting to find treasure. But they were full of rubbish – old books and papers, rotting Arab saddles and empty medicine bottles.

The Princess and the Pirates

She dazzled society and captivated Napoleon

One April evening in 1817 a clergyman in the village of Almondsbury, Gloucestershire, opened his cottage door to find a young woman outside. She was modestly dressed in a plain black frock with a high, ruffled neck but her hair was swathed in a black turban and she babbled incoherently in a language he did not understand.

Since she was obviously exhausted, he let her rest for a while before sending for the village overseer, who dealt with all the waifs and strays who turned up in the Parish. He too was completely baffled.

Eventually the two men bundled her into a carriage and set off for Knole

Park, home of local magistrate and landowner, Samuel Worrall.

At the sight of the fine mansion, the strange girl became terrified and only after a fierce struggle could she be persuaded to go inside. It was Mrs Worrall, a kind, motherly woman, who eventually managed to calm the stranger.

She was an enchanting creature, her head small and neat, her eyes black and limpid. When she smiled her soft, full lips parted to show dazzling white teeth and when she became excited, a rosy flush spread over her dusky skin. Her hands were delicate and apparently unaccustomed to hard work. She appeared to be about 25 years old.

It was decided to send her, with a maid, to sleep for the night in the village inn. Supper was laid on a table, but she refused to touch it. When the landlord brought tea, however, she seized the cup greedily, covered her eyes and gabbled some kind of prayer.

When the landlord's wife took her to her room, she stubbornly refused to get into bed and indicated that she would rather curl up on the floor. It was only when the landlord's small daughter bounced encouragingly up and down on the feather mattress that she at last consented to lie down and go to sleep.

The following morning Mrs Worrall arrived at the inn to find the young woman sitting disconsolately by the fire. She jumped up, greeted her with joy and clung to her hand possessively. There seemed no alternative but to take her back to Knole Park, where breakfast was laid. It was Good Friday and freshly baked hot cross buns were on the table. The girl reached out and took one, then to everyone's amazement, cut off the cross with a knife and stuffed it in the bodice of her dress. Could she be a Christian?

When Mrs Worrall later returned from church, she marched up to her 'guest', looked her in the eye and said 'My good young woman, I very much fear that you are imposing on me and that you can understand and answer me in my own language....'

The girl gazed back, uncomprehending.

'If so,' she went on, 'and distress has driven you to this, make a friend of me. I will give you money and clothes and put you on your journey without disclosing your conduct to anyone – but it must be on condition that you speak the truth.'

Still there was no sign of understanding.

Suddenly Mrs Worrall had a brainwave. Thumping herself on the chest, she called out 'Worrall! Worrall!' After several repeats of this performance the girl grinned from ear to ear and pointing to herself shouted 'Caraboo! Caraboo!'

For the next 10 weeks Caraboo ruled the roost. The Worralls were

'Princess Caraboo'

besieged by curious friends and acquaintances, many of them bringing foreign visitors. Among them was a Portuguese from Malaya, who triumphantly announced that Caraboo was a Princess. She had been kidnapped by pirates and brought to England against her will. Her language was a mixture of dialects used on the coast of Sumatra!

Her admirers were enormously impressed. But it was another widely travelled friend of the Worralls who, using signs, gestures and a smattering of the words she seemed to know, finally extracted her remarkable, vividly detailed story. She came, he said, from the island of Javasu in the East Indies. Her father, Jessu Mandu, was a high-caste Chinese of such awesome authority that people had to make obeisance to him on both knees. He was carried about on the shoulders of macratoos (common men) in a kind of sedan chair and wore a nugget of gold with three peacock feathers in his headdress. He had four wives, and Caraboo's mother, the favourite, was a beautiful Malay who blackened her teeth and wore jewels in her nose.

Caraboo had been walking in the garden one day with three sammen (serving maids) when she was seized by the crew of a pirate ship. Her father swam after the marauding party, but after a fight the raiders won the day; she was bound hand and foot and carried off to sea.

After 11 days, the pirate chief sold her to the captain of a brig named Tappa Boo, a terrifying man with black whiskers, greasy black hair worn in a plait and an evil eye. His perpetual smile scared her out of her wits.

After several months at sea, the brig reached northern waters and skirted the coast of England. One night, in desperation, Caraboo jumped overboard and swam for shore.

At the time she had been wearing a dress of finest silk worked with gold. She dried it in the sun and soon after, meeting a village girl in the fields, exchanged it for a simple black frock and shawl, which she wound round her head like a turban. For six weeks she roamed the countryside, begging for food and sleeping in barns and hayricks until, one night, she reached Almondsbury.

Deeply impressed, the Worrall household settled down to living with their royal guest.

She cut the most unlikely figure on the lawns of an English country house. From a length of calico she made herself a dress with sleeves so wide and long they trailed on the ground. Her feet were bare and her head was decorated with feathers and flowers.

Sometimes she carried a gong which she struck loudly and often, and sometimes she would bang on a tambourine. Armed with a bow and arrow, she would stalk about the place like Diana, goddess of the hunt.

They allowed her to prepare her own food. She was particularly fond of rice and hot vegetable curries, but ate little meat and drank only water and tea. She refused to eat pigeon cooked in the kitchen, but picked up a live one, cut off its head, burying this in the ground, then roasted and ate the rest of it.

She seemed strongly religious. When shown a drawing of an idol from the South Seas she threw it to the ground and made it clear that she worshipped Allah-Tallah – the true God. She said her prayers night and morning, made a temple in the shrubbery and every Tuesday perched on the steep roof at Knole, praying until sunset.

As the weeks went by the Worralls' nerves became a little ragged. No one knew quite what she would do next. Passionately fond of bathing, she once plunged into the lake fully dressed. She would also wash her face in the fish pond.

Then, suddenly, it was all over. One June night Caraboo stole away. She did not take a pin that did not belong to her. All her gifts and trinkets were left in a neat pile in her room.

Weeks went by. After enquiries Mrs Worrall learned that her protégée had turned up in Bath and set off in pursuit.

Hearing that Caraboo had been taken up by a fashionable society woman, she burst into a tea party and found the girl being courted by a horde of elegant admirers. When she saw Mrs W. she sank gracefully to her knees, begging forgiveness, saying she had run away to find someone who would help her return to her homeland.

The determined Mrs Worrall took her back to Gloucestershire. But the bubble was about to burst.

Glowing descriptions of the exotic stranger began to appear in various newspapers, including the *Bristol Journal*. A lodging house keeper called Mrs Neale, coming across the story of the Princess from Javasu, decided it rang a bell. Caraboo sounded very much like a fanciful young woman who had stayed with her some months before ... very much like her.

Mrs Neale was eventually brought face to face with Caraboo in Mrs Worrall's presence. Without hesitation, she exclaimed, 'That's Mary Baker!'

Caraboo burst into tears. She admitted that she was in fact the daughter of a poor Devon cobbler and had never in her life set foot in a foreign country.

Her story is told in a slender pamphlet published in 1817 under the title *Caraboo – a Narrative of a Singular Imposition Practiced Upon the Benevolence of a Lady*. It draws a picture of a delightful eccentric.

Caraboo was born Mary Wilcocks in the village of Witheridge, near Crediton, Devonshire, in 1791. Her parents were poor, respectable people with too many children. She received little education and ran wild until she was eight years old, when she was taught spinning.

At 16 her parents found her a steady job at a nearby farmhouse, looking after the farmer's children and doing manual work. But her head was full of dreams. On her days off she pretended to be a Spanish or French woman. Once she dressed up as a gypsy and looked so authentic her employers did not recognize her.

After two years of earning ten pence a week she asked for a rise. The farmer refused to pay her any more so she went back home. Her furious father thrashed her with a leather strap. It was more than her wild spirit could take. She ran away.

Once, between jobs, she lived with a tribe of gypsies, slept in barns and begged for food. The rough life did not suit her. She became desperately ill and was taken to St Giles Hospital, London, where she almost died.

After recovering, she found a good position with a Mr Matthews and his wife who lived in a handsome house in Clapham Place. Her employer taught her to read properly and to write, allowing her to use his library. She spent all her leisure time devouring books that described life in far-off lands, exotic customs and romantic adventures.

After three years she was dismissed and became a vagabond again. For a time she protected herself from the robbers and murderers who roamed the heaths around London by dressing in male breeches and jacket, cutting off her hair and passing herself off as a young man.

Back in petticoats, she became a servant to a fishmonger's wife in Dark House Lane, Billingsgate. Only one thing made the job bearable: she was sent out regularly on errands. In a bookshop she caught the eye of a well-dressed foreigner. Introducing himself as Herr Bakerstendht (which she shortened to Baker), he told her he had travelled widely in the East and soon declared his love for her. After two months she went through a form of marriage with him. Soon he told her he had to travel to Calais on business and would send for her later. Of course she never saw him again.

From then on she retired into her fantasy world: eventually she became Princess Caraboo of Javasu.

There were red faces when the truth became known. But people admitted she was a remarkable young woman and were curious to meet her. She was visited by all sorts of people, including linguists, who were dying to know how she had kept up the deception.

Her 'language' had been made up mostly of Malay and Arabic words which she had learned from 'Mr Baker', plus a smattering of Romany picked up from the gypsies; and her knowledge of life in the East had come only from books.

When the good-hearted Mrs Worrall had got over her shock she agreed to help the Devonshire 'princess'. Mary longed to go to America. The magistrate's wife fitted her out with clothes, gave her some money and booked her passage on board a ship leaving Bristol, putting her in charge of a group of missionaries.

That is not quite the end of the story. The *Bristol Journal* of September 13, 1817, carried a letter from Sir Hudson Lowe, governor of Napoleon's prison island, St Helena.

Apparently, one day during a storm, Sir Hudson saw a ship tacking offshore. The wind proved too strong and he watched it bear away to the north-west. Shortly afterwards a small boat, bobbing like a cork, was seen entering the harbour. Sir Hudson went down to the beach and watched a 'female of interesting appearance' scramble ashore. It was Mary Baker.

She had felt, she explained, an 'ardent desire' to see Napoleon. When she realized they were not going to land at St Helena, she cut loose a lifeboat and rowed for the shore.

Sir Hudson introduced her to Napoleon as Princess Caraboo and apparently she carried on her performance as though there had been no interval. Napoleon was completely captivated and asked that she might be allowed an apartment in his house....

Mary Baker clearly had a genius for making men believe what they wanted to believe. How her affair with Napoleon ended we do not know. That was the last heard of her. But there was a rumour, years later, that she had been seen in London, selling leeches.

Chapter
Three

BARMY BUILDERS

Some eccentrics never feel satisfied unless they have
made their mark in bricks and mortar. That's why the
landscapes of the world are littered with amazing
architectural follies . . . like the one that took 500
labourers six years to build and came crashing down at
the first gust of strong wind . . . and the amazing stately
home that was built entirely underground . . .

Ups and downs of Beckford's Towers

His buildings reached for the sky, but crashed to the ground

William Beckford had a passion for building towers – the higher the better. But his talents were more suited to the role of demolition expert. Whatever he put up was as likely as not to come tumbling down.

In 1795 he set an army of labourers to work on what became known as the greatest architectural 'folly' in England – the tower of Fonthill Abbey at his family estate near Hindon, in Wiltshire.

It soared to 300 feet, competing with the spire of Salisbury Cathedral. But at the first powerful gust of wind it swayed, snapped in two and came crashing to the ground.

Beckford said his only regret was that he had not been present to see the spectacle.

Everything this brilliant, impulsive man did had to be finished in a hurry. Even his considerable acts of generosity had to be rushed through before he could change his mind.

He had been used to getting his own way since childhood. The son of a wealthy businessman who was twice Lord Mayor of London, he was brought up in an atmosphere of princely luxury. He studied Arabic and Persian under famous Oriental scholars, took piano lessons from Mozart and was taught architecture by Sir William Chambers, designer of London's Somerset House.

When his father died in 1770 Beckford was only 10 years old, but he inherited £1,000,000 in cash, property in England and vast sugar plantations in Jamaica. His income was £100,000 a year – a fantastic sun for the 18th century.

Most of his youth was spent travelling abroad with a retinue of servants, including his own musicians. At one time he kept an elderly mistress in Venice who, it was said, had been a lover of Casanova.

But Beckford's days were not spent in idleness. He was a prolific writer. Books poured from his pen. When he was 21 he produced a masterpiece, a highly original Oriental romance, *Vathek*. Typically, it was done in a hurry. He wrote it in French at a single sitting of three days and two nights.

'I never took off my clothes the whole time,' he said. 'This severe application made me very ill.'

He revelled in everything mysterious or strange and was inspired by the great medieval monasteries and cathedrals he saw on his travels, especially in Spain and Portugal.

These were to be his blueprint when, in 1795, after years of wandering, a tragically short marriage and a scandal involving a handsome boy, Beckford cut himself off from society and settled at his family estate at Fonthill.

He decided to build a Gothic abbey, a private folly on a scale unknown in England, with a colossal tower as its main feature.

Before work began, he had a wall built around his estate to keep out sightseers and neighbours. It was 12 feet high and 7 miles long. He hired a leading architect, James Wyatt, and work was immediately started on the great tower. Beckford had already boasted that he intended to live in the tallest private residence in England, and he did not care how much it cost him. Cynics sneered that he was merely building a monument to himself.

The truth was, Beckford had building in his blood and wanted to see his romantic fantasies translated into reality.

His impatience was obvious from the start. He would not wait for proper foundations to be dug. He insisted that those that had already been laid for a small summer house would do. The builders protested, but he ordered them to carry on, totally ignoring the architect's plans.

Loud protests were also made about the materials he used. Instead of stone or brick he insisted on timber and cement, because they could be worked more quickly.

He employed 500 labourers to work in two shifts, half by day, half by torchlight. At one point, when he thought things were slowing down, Beckford enticed 460 men away from building St George's Chapel at Windsor. Unfortunately, he also stepped up their ale ration to encourage their efforts, so that a great deal of the tower was built by labourers almost too drunk to see the wall in front of them.

Local farmers complained bitterly when he commandeered every cart and wagon in the district to carry building materials. The farms were brought to a standstill. But Beckford also used those same carts to deliver free coal and to distribute hundreds of blankets to the poor in bitter weather.

Six years after it had been begun, the tower, with all its pinnacles and weather vanes was complete, and Beckford was not the only one to heave a sigh of relief.

Then down it came with a roar like thunder.

Not a man to waste emotion, he immediately gave orders for the building of a new tower on the rubble of the old. Stone was added to make it stronger and it was finished within a relatively leisurely seven years.

The abbey itself was a dazzling affair of medieval grandeur. The great halls and galleries were decorated in red, gold and purple. Everywhere was the gleam of silver. But the bedrooms were all dark, tiny and badly ventilated and most of the time only one was occupied – that in which Beckford slept in monastic simplicity. He was attended by a Spanish dwarf in full livery.

Beckford seldom admitted visitors to his retreat, but every day his dining table was laid for 12 people. The kitchens would prepare food for 12 and footmen would stand to attention behind each chair. But he dined alone, eating a single dish and sending the others away.

Only once while he lived at Fonthill was the full glory of the abbey seen by outsiders. This was in 1800 when Lord Nelson and Lady Hamilton were chief guests at a magnificent reception. Beckford's biographer, Cyrus Redding, describes how the company was escorted from Fonthill House to the abbey by a military band playing solemn airs and marches. The road wound through thick woods of pine and fir, illuminated by numberless lamps suspended in the trees. Suddenly Beckford's folly loomed before them and they fell silent with stunned admiration as lights blazed on soaring walls, battlements and turrets.

They were led into a great salon hung with rare tapestries, and sat on ebony chairs at tables laid with ivory. Dinner was served from enormous silver dishes in the manner of a medieval banquet. Tall wax candles flickered in silver sconces and monk-like, hooded figures stood in attendance. Everyone was mesmerized by the experience.

Beckford had vowed that he would eat Christmas dinner only if it had been cooked in the new abbey kitchens. He was warned that they could not be built in time. But he had made up his mind and his workmen knew they would have to beat the clock.

On Christmas morning fires were lit in the great ovens and the cooks began preparing the feast. They tried to forget that the bricks had not had time to settle, that the beams had not been secured and that the mortar was scarcely dry.

Beckford's dinner was served, but even as servants were hurrying along the passages which led from the kitchens to the dining room, there was an enormous crash.

The kitchens had caved in.

Eventually, tower, kitchens and all were rebuilt and Beckford lived on his Fonthill estate until 1822 when a slump in the sugar market – the main source of his wealth – badly affected his financial position.

He was forced to sell.

For the first time the abbey was open to public view and thousands flocked to see it. Eventually his beloved folly was sold for £330,000 to an ammunitions dealer, John Farquhar.

Perhaps Farquhar had not noticed that the famous tower was in a dubious state of health. He had hardly had time to explore his newly acquired property when the inevitable happened. One night in a roaring gale the whole thing came crashing down again.

Meanwhile Beckford had purchased two delightful houses in the famous spa town of Bath. They were separated by a mews and he decided to link them with a bridge. He furnished the twin houses with all the choicest things he had brought away from Fonthill. It was perfect, but for one detail – there was no tower.

He employed a young Bath architect to design a high retreat for him on the rocky slope where his property stood. Between the tower and the houses he laid gardens, importing fully grown trees and transforming its entire surroundings.

But he had learned his lesson. For once he was not in a hurry – and he was content for the tower to be only 130 feet high. He lived to enjoy it for 20 years, dying peacefully in 1844 at the age of 84.

And Beckford's tower still stands in Bath today.

Fonthill Abbey

Ornamental hermit

The earl's son who craved romance

The 18th-century landowner, Charles Hamilton, advertised for a hermit to live in a specially built hermitage on his estate at Pain's Hill, Cobham, in Surrey. He did not fancy being one himself, but rather admired the species. Besides, he felt that an 'ornamental hermit', as Edith Sitwell later called him, would add to the romantic atmosphere of his magnificent park.

The Hon. Charles, youngest son of the sixth Earl of Abercorn, had laid out at Pain's Hill what proved to be one of the finest examples of natural landscape gardening in England. When he bought the land, around 1738, it was nothing more than a barren heath, a dreary, sandy moorland that most people thought not worth cultivating. First he burned the heather, and then he grew a fine crop of turnips which were fed to flocks of sheep which manured the ground so well that it was soon covered by a fine crop of grass.

He moved tons of earth to make hills and valleys and created a lake by pumping water from the River Mole. Having studied romantic Italian painting, he decided that was how he wanted his Park to look. He built a modest house for himself, then spent every available penny on the 400 acres surrounding it. As far as the eye could see there were great vistas of naturally growing cedars, oaks, elms and beeches; spectacular flowering shrubs were imported from all over the world, including, for the first time, great seas of rhododendrons, never before planted on such a scale in England.

Amidst all this natural grandeur were Hamilton's follies. Modelling himself as closely as possible on the romantic paintings he had seen, he dotted them all over the place. There was a stucco and wood Gothic temple, which the purists said was anything but Gothic; a Chinese bridge, an octagonal Turkish tent, a temple of Bacchus made from papier-mâché, a medieval gazebo, a ruined abbey, a castle tower and a great Roman arch. Then, tucked away in a gloomy dell, he created the hermitage. It was perfect but for one thing. It needed a hermit.

The dell was part of a steep mound. There was an upper apartment where the hermit could sit, cross-legged or otherwise. This was supported partly by the contorted roots of trees, which formed the entrance to the cell.

Charles Hamilton's rules were very strict. His hermit, he explained, must

Charles Hamilton

49

be prepared to stay for seven years. He would be supplied with a mat on which to sleep and a hassock for resting his head and praying. He would also be provided with a Bible, a pair of optical glasses (spectacles) and an hourglass as a timepiece. Water and food would be brought to him from the house, but on no account was he to exchange a word with the servants. Mr Hamilton himself would not address the hermit at any time. Ordinary clothes were not allowed and the hermit would have to agree to wear a camel's-hair robe, which, though uncomfortable and scratchy, was traditional. Never under any circumstances would he be allowed to cut his hair, beard or nails. While permitted a stroll in the Park, he must never stray beyond the boundary of Pain's Hill.

If the wretched man remained in the hermitage without breaking one of these conditions for the full seven years, he would receive a reward of £700. But if he broke even one of the conditions laid down, he would not receive a penny.

One optimistic hermit did turn up, don the camel's-hair robe and take residence. But three weeks in that gloomy place was enough for him. He slipped away in the night without asking for a penny.

The whole affair infuriated Horace Walpole, that great deflator of other people's high-flown ideas. He snorted that it was ridiculous to allow a quarter of one's garden to be used merely for someone else to be melancholy in it.

Nevertheless, Hamilton's estate was regarded as a work of art and himself as something of a genius. People came from near and far to drive round it and to row across the lake to an island where he had created the most exquisite grotto. They also visited his vineyard where he produced a splendid sparkling white wine which sold for 7s 6d a bottle.

Then, after spending half a lifetime creating his idyllic 'living picture', he was forced to put it up for sale. By 1775 the expense had proved too much for his pocket. Though the son of an Earl he was ninth in line and not particularly rich.

He retired to Bath and continued to advise other people, whose gardens became famous. Pain's Hill is still there, but it has suffered from neglect and Hamilton's follies are long forgotten.

The Duke who detested daylight

He built fifteen miles of tunnel under his estate

Like a mole hiding from the light of day, William John Cavendish Bentinck Scott, fifth Duke of Portland, vanished underground when he inherited Welbeck Abbey in the 'Dukeries' country of Nottinghamshire.

Welbeck had always lain too low for most members of the Portland family. But it was not low enough for William John who, after coming into the title in 1854, spent the rest of his life burrowing.

He hated meeting people and never invited anyone to his home – yet he set out to construct a vast complex of subterranean rooms which included the largest ballroom in the country, a 250-ft library, a huge glass-roofed conservatory and a billiard-room big enough to take a dozen billiard tables.

He was mad about tunnels. There were 15 miles of them running underneath his park linking the buried rooms with the rest of the Abbey and with each other. One tunnel, a mile and quarter long, ran from his coach-house to Worksop, enabling him to come and go unseen when he had a sudden whim to catch the London train. It was wide enough to take two carriages and was eerily lit by domed skylights during the day and hundreds of gas jets by night.

The story of this lonely, eccentric Duke, who was seldom seen by anyone but builders during his lifetime, is one of the strangest to be found in the history of the British aristocracy.

Born in 1800, he lived what appeared to be a reasonably normal life as a young man, frequenting London society, holding commissions in fashionable regiments and even, for a short period, representing Kings Lynn in Parliament. But he was awkward in the company of women and a confirmed bachelor. And gradually, his acute shyness, apparently inherited from his mother, took over his whole personality.

From the moment he moved into Welbeck until he died, he went to the most extraordinary lengths to avoid contact with people. He stripped the great rooms of the abbey of all their fine tapestries, carpets, furniture and ancestral portraits, and stowed them out of sight in a jumbled heap. Then he

51

retreated to four or five sparsely furnished rooms tucked away in the west wing, and it was here that he worked out his plans for burrowing.

The door of each room had a double letter-box, one for incoming, one for outgoing, notes. His valet seemed to be the only servant allowed near him. When he fell ill and needed medical care, the doctor would be asked to stand outside while the valet took the Duke's pulse and reported his condition.

Such secrecy led to the wildest rumours. Some said that he had a hideous skin disease and was not fit to be seen. Others felt sure he had gone raving mad. But in fact a photograph which he had allowed to be taken in typical Victorian style with his gloves and tall hat on a table by his side, show that he was a pleasant-looking man with a wide, generous mouth, large nose and mutton-chop whiskers. Mr F. J. Turner, the resident agent at Welbeck, who must have come into contact with his employer at some time, told the fifth Duke that he was 'extremely handsome, kind and clever'.

For years he was completely absorbed in building his underground rooms and tunnels. There was no comfort anywhere. The whole place looked like a mammoth construction site with mountains of builders' rubble, wheelbarrows and shovels all over the ancestral pile. His passion for bricks and mortar may well have been inherited from his distant ancestor, Bess of Hardwick, the formidable Elizabethan lady who built some of the greatest houses in England and who acquired Welbeck Abbey for the family in the first place.

Everything he did was on an enormous scale. Hundreds of workmen were employed at a time. The underground ballroom alone measured 174 feet long and 64 feet wide and had an hydraulic lift able to carry 20 guests at a time from the surface. Two thousand people could have danced with ease under giant chandeliers and a ceiling painted to resemble a glowing sunset.

Why did this lonely man build a ballroom? Presumably, in his heart the Duke longed to be a different kind of creature altogether – a man who gave parties and balls and received his guests with lavish hospitality. But he never summoned up the courage.

The Duke was said at one time to be one of the best judges of horseflesh in England and his stables at Welbeck held nearly 100 horses, none of which he ever rode. The buildings above ground included a windowless riding school, the second largest in the world, lit by 4,000 gas jets.

For some obscure reason he ordered all the great, bare unused rooms in the Abbey to be painted in a most unsubtle shade of pink and in the corner of each, exposed to full view, was installed a lavatory basin.

As work progressed at Welbeck he was sometimes forced to come into contact with his workmen. But they were given firm orders. On no account must they show by any sign that they had recognized him. If a man touched

William John Cavendish Bentinck Scott, fifth Duke of Portland

his cap in deference, he was dismissed. His tenants were told to pass him by 'as if he was a tree'.

The only time he would venture out for a walk was in the dead of night when a woman servant carrying a lantern was sent 40 yards ahead of him, with strict orders not to speak or look behind.

He had a most peculiar style of dressing. Sometimes on sweltering hot summer days he was glimpsed wearing a full-length sable coat. On other occasions he put on three frock-coats of different sizes, all at once, one on top of the other. His trousers were tied up with a length of old string, just above the ankles. Whatever the weather, he carried with him an old umbrella and a heavy topcoat. If someone approached and looked likely to address him, he would immediately cover himself with the coat and snap up the umbrella to hide his face. He took to wearing a dark brown wig – he had boxes of them in his bedroom – and on top of it he would perch a stove pipe hat, nearly two feet high.

His daily diet was chicken, always chicken. For years he had one killed every morning and roasted on the spit in the kitchens above ground. When ready it would be lowered by lift into a heated truck which ran on rails through one of the underground tunnels and into the house.

In spite of his strange behaviour he was a good and thoughtful employer. His workmen were paid good wages and were given, in addition, an umbrella to protect them from the rain and a donkey on which to ride to work.

In the 'pleasure garden' at Welbeck there was a large skating rink and a man was employed specifically to look after the skates of every size that were kept there. The Duke had decided that it would be good for his domestic staff to have regular exercise and housemaids were sent skating daily, whether they liked it or not.

The farms, schools and roads on his estate were kept in excellent condition and his greenhouses were among the finest in the country. He laid down avenues of fruit trees and a huge vegetable garden.

When the Duke decided to go up to London, his departure was contrived with the utmost secrecy. He would leave Welbeck via the underground tunnel in a black hearse-like carriage, drawn by black horses. Green silk blinds completely covered the windows. He would remain seated in the carriage while it was loaded onto a railway truck at Worksop station, and he would not leave it for the entire journey. When he arrived at Harcourt House, his London residence in Cavendish Square, all the servants would be ordered out of sight while he climbed down and hurried through the front hall and into his study.

Precautions were taken to ensure his absolute privacy by erecting screens all round the garden. For years his neighbours had been tortured with curiosity and most were convinced that orgies were taking place.

Welbeck Abbey was in a state of utter chaos when he suddenly died in his 80th year in December 1879. His cousin, arriving with his family in a carriage to take up the inheritance, found the drive overgrown with tangled weeds and grasses, and strewn with rubble. Planks had to be fetched to ease the carriage over the debris. When the great front door was thrown open, the sixth Duke was staggered to see that the hall had no floor. He went on to discover the strange pink rooms with the lavatories, and then to find all the treasures of Welbeck stuffed away like worthless bric-a-brac, the tapestries in tin trunks, the ancestral portraits stacked against the wall without their frames.

But the world had not yet finished with the fifth Duke. He had been buried with the utmost simplicity and his grave tucked away in a shrubbery at Kensal Green cemetery in North London when the whispers started.

Had the Duke been leading a double life? Nothing could have been easier for him. His comings and goings were always secretive and few people knew what he really looked like. Rumours had been going round London for years.

It all came to a head in the 'Druce Affair', which provided English society with enough gossip for a decade. A widow named Anna Maria Druce, who lived at 68 Baker Street, London, claimed that the late Duke had been none other then her beloved husband, Thomas Charles Druce, owner of a flourishing shop called the Baker Street Bazaar.

Druce was thought to have died in 1864. But his 'widow' swore that the funeral at Highgate cemetery had been a mockery. The coffin had been filled with lead.

It was, she claimed, no more than a ruse to allow her husband, who had grown tired of his alter ego, to return to his reclusive but aristocratic life at Welbeck. She therefore claimed the title and lands of the Portland family for her son.

The sixth Duke treated the claim with 'supreme contempt' but enough speculators were found to put up £30,000 in an attempt to fight the case, which dragged on for years.

When it eventually came to court, the Druce family and their supporters committed perjury so many times that the case became a national joke. Eventually in 1907 it was decided to open the alleged Thomas Druce's grave in Highgate. He was found lying there 'aged and bearded' and perfectly at peace.

The case collapsed, the tricksters were sent packing and the fifth Duke was allowed to sink back at last into the obscurity that he had so passionately desired.

Castle Curious

The do-it-yourself master-builder
from County Cork

Irishman Johnny Roche built himself a castle in County Cork with nothing more in the way of tools than a spade, a shovel and a rickety old cart.

For three years – from 1867 to 1870 – he sweated and laboured, gathering stones from the river by hand, digging away furiously, and drawing lime in his ancient cart pulled by an equally ancient donkey.

As the castle grew higher and higher he invented a winch to draw up the stones. People came from miles around to stare. They called it 'Castle Curious' and obviously thought its builder mighty curious too.

Johnny Roche dressed in loose, flowing garments spun and stitched by himself, with a wide-brimmed hat pulled low to conceal his bearded face. His passion to possess a castle of his own, when he had hardly two pennies to rub together, convinced the locals he was mad.

They knew him as the son of a carpenter and blacksmith from Walltown, near Mallow, who had emigrated to America to make his fortune, but returned empty-handed. Back in Cork he had tried running a mill beside the Awbeg river and when that failed, turned his hand to making tombstones. Building castles seemed right out of his league.

But when the strange building with its labyrinth of tiny rooms was finished, Johnny Roche confounded them all by moving in and living there for the rest of his life.

Today the labyrinth is in ruins, but the framework still stands. It consists of an oval tower 45 feet high and 27 feet in length, topped by two oval turrets that run at right-angles to the main building. At the base of the tower a slab of granite is engraved with fine lettering: John Roche, 1870.

In his lifetime one of the turrets carried a flag with a flying angel, and the walls were ornamented with gargoyles. He did not encourage callers and, thanks to a private well inside the castle walls, was able to 'pull up his drawbridge' whenever he felt inclined. St Bernard's Holy Well, however, lay only a few feet from the castle walls and Johnny Roche, afraid that his privacy was threatened, would lean out of a tower window and rain down colourful abuse on the heads of pilgrims.

He was, however, by no means a recluse. He travelled about the countryside on a home-made bicycle or else in a ramshackle coach drawn by two mules and equipped with a bed and a stove.

His skills developed as he grew older. It was said he could draw teeth, mend clocks, produce sculpture, play the bagpipes and the violin, dance, whistle and sing.

His best friend, a retired dragoon called Nixon, was so impressed by his talents that he asked Roche to design his tombstone if he should die first. In due course the master builder erected a flagpole over the grave of his friend with the bare inscription 'HERE LIES NIXON'. He planned something more elaborate for himself, but died before he could order his plans to be carried out. However, his own epitaph survives:

'Here lies the body of poor John Roche.
He had his faults, but don't reproach;
For while alive his heart was mellow;
An artist, genius and gentle fellow.'

Chapter Four

MADLY IN LOVE

The pleasure and pain of love has driven men and women to extremes of eccentric behaviour. They let nothing stand in their way . . . like the prince who fell simultaneously in love with a mother and her two daughters . . . and the great Casanova who consumed feasts of supposedly aphrodisiac oysters set out upon the naked bodies of his paramours . . .

The amorous Prince Pickle

Passionate letters – to be used again if required

For the wildly romantic German aristocrat, Prince Pückler-Muskau, falling in love was as necessary as breathing. It was said that he fell for 'every petticoat that crossed his path' but even more remarkable was his vast correspondence. After his death a whole library of love letters was discovered, most of them in high-flown French, all carefully preserved and pulsating with adoration, ecstasy or despair. Rough copies of every letter were marked 'To be used again if required'.

The ardent prince had a magnetic vitality and his deep blue eyes seemed to mesmerize his victims. Jealous rivals, however, spread the rumour that he was often paralyzed by shyness when it came to proving his ardour.

Pückler was a gifted author, an adventurous traveller and one of the greatest landscape gardeners in Europe. But love crept into everything he did. Thus, he fell passionately in love with his English translator, Sara Austin, without even meeting her. The poor woman, married with a child, was virtually seduced by post: 'Last night I had a dream of you, a rapturous dream – oh it was life itself! I pressed your lovely form in delirious madness to my heart, and thought to feel your burning kisses on my thirsty lips....' On and on raved Pückler until Sara was prostrate with guilt and nervous exhaustion.

His Highness Hermann Ludwig Heinrich Pückler-Muskau, only son of Graf von Pückler and his child bride Clementine, endured a wretched and lonely childhood. He was born in October 1785 when his mother, a frivolous little flirt, was only 15. His father coldly ignored him. His only companions were servants and estate workers.

At the age of 15 he fell in love with his mother, now a mature and fascinating woman, who after divorcing the Graf had remarried, yet often returned to her old home at Muskau with her new husband in tow. Her son's adolescent agonies touched her vanity and she did nothing to discourage him. He suffered painfully.

At Leipzig University, reading Law, he spent most of his time gambling and discovering the joys of wild living. Naturally he plunged into debt and the hands of the money-lenders.

Law, he decided, was a bore, so he ran off to Dresden where he joined a crack cavalry regiment and was very soon promoted to Captain of the Horse. Once, to impress a young woman, he took a flying leap on his horse over the parapet of a bridge and into the rushing waters of the River Elbe. On another occasion, he galloped up the steps of a casino, played and won at the tables without dismounting, then galloped down again.

Finally his debts became too pressing. In 1804 he threw up his commission and went to live more modestly in Vienna. When his disapproving father drastically reduced his allowance, young Pückler started to pay off his creditors, dismissed his servant, sold his carriage, gold watch and sword, and rented an attic. There he lived in semi-starvation, unable to afford fuel even in the bitterest weather.

When the time came for the obligatory Grand Tour of Europe, his father would still not relent. So Pückler set off through Switzerland, Italy and France with a pack on his pack. He stayed at the humblest inns and made friends with tramps and vagabonds. It gave him a yearning for travel that lasted all his life.

In 1811, the Graf died and the huge estates of Muskau in Silesia, with its 45 villages and its own court of justice, fell into his lap. He hated the place. It was set in bleak, monotonous country on barren soil. How could he change it?

He set to work with ferocious energy. When finished, Muskau was to become one of the showplaces of Europe, a marvel of imaginative landscape design.

Pückler did nothing by halves. He removed a whole village from the right to the left bank of the River Neisse, created hills and valleys, transported thousands of fully grown trees to forest the barren terrain, and blew up anything he didn't like. He deflected the river to create streams, lakes, waterfalls and cataracts. Having discovered a spring of mineral water, he built a pump room, a theatre and a casino, and called the place Hermannsbad. But it was no conventional spa. Pückler didn't believe in wheelchairs. He staged steeplechases, illuminations, fireworks and theatrical spectaculars as part of the cure.

He decided to get married. Typically, not one woman but *three* caught his fancy. Worse, they all belonged to the same family. His heart fluttered between Lucie, Countess of Pappenheim, a well-preserved blonde of 40, her natural daughter, Adelheid, and her adopted daughter, Helmine. Friends assured him that marriage to the mother would make the most stir. She was nine years older than he, about to be divorced, and the daughter of Prince Hardenberg, Chancellor of Prussia; in fact, quite a catch.

Pückler proposed to Lucie and was joyfully accepted. But panic set in as he saw matrimony approaching. He suddenly found himself madly in love with Lucie's sylph-like daughter, Adelheid, and wondered for one insane moment whether they could not have a three-way arrangement. Lucie said 'No' very firmly.

He got over Adelheid only to fall passionately in love with 16-year-old Helmine. They managed to get him through the wedding, which was celebrated with processions and fireworks, but when it came to leaving for Paris on the honeymoon he used the most hilarious delaying tactics so as not to have to leave Helmine behind.

The Pücklers had one overwhelming interest in common – to turn Muskau from a dull backwater estate into an earthly paradise. They plotted and planned and spent money like water. The sandy soil soaked up a fortune and neither bothered to count the cost. Nine years after their marriage they were faced with financial ruin.

Lucie suggested a startling solution. They must get a divorce. Pückler could then set out to find an heiress with enough money to rescue them from disaster – and save Muskau.

Astonishingly, they went through with it and after the divorce hearing in 1826 collapsed into each other's arms in floods of tears.

Pückler went off to England where, he had heard, heiresses were thick on the ground. For three years he made the social round, flirting with famous beauties, dining with royalty and paying as many as 50 calls in a morning.

Like the Dandies, he wore frock coats of exquisite cut, the finest shirts and almost effeminate jewellery. He surveyed the scene through an eyeglass fixed to the top of his cane and dyed his hair black to make himself look younger.

Many people decided he was a rogue; others were amused and called him 'Prince Pickle'. But he was no good as a fortune hunter. His timing was unfortunate, his strategy hopeless and his despair, in the letters he sent home to Lucie, almost comic.

Though unable to scoop up an heiress, he did find time to declare his undying love for the exquisite little opera singer Henriette Sontag, who had become the toast of London. The besotted prince sold a diamond buckle to raise the 80 guineas demanded for a box at her concert. She soon came to her senses and returned to her fiancé. He decided to take his broken heart back to Muskau.

Lucie continued to live with him as platonic soulmate. Pückler placed a gilded bust of Henriette in his garden and began writing a book about his recent experiences. It proved an enormous success, but some of its honest observations on class distinctions caused a rumpus in England where it was translated by Sara Austin as *The Tour of a German Prince*.

His postal wooing of Sara helped him to forget Henriette. There was also a

The amorous Prince Pückler-Muskau

beautiful Eurasian to comfort him nearer home and after her a succession of charming and witty creatures, all anxious to smooth his brow.

But he bit off more than he could chew when he accepted the flattery of an intellectual lady, Bettina von Arnim. She had been Goethe's mistress and made a habit of falling in love with famous men. At 60 she was old enough to be Pückler's mother and he squirmed with embarrassment at her coy antics. Eventually she made him look so ridiculous he had to tell her to leave him alone. She took the hint and agreed to a 'communion of souls'.

Since writing brought him in sufficient income, Pückler decided to pack his bags and see more of the world. He set off in style, travelling in a smart black coupé trimmed with yellow, a green parrot in a cage, a little dog at his feet and a lorgnette languidly raised to survey the passing landscape. He wore a black military frock coat, a brilliant cashmere shawl and a red fez with a blue tassel.

He was away for years exploring Africa and living with the Bedouin. He travelled up the Nile with an entourage that included a doctor, a bodyguard, a valet, a Greek page called Janni, two little slave boys, an Arab chef who had learned French cooking and a miniature harem composed of two nubile Abyssinian girls. He rode through the desert on a dromedary from Wadi Halfa to Dongola, and pressed on southwards as far as Khartoum before contracting dysentery and being forced to return to Alexandria.

Of course, he found beautiful women to adore in Algiers, Tunis, Crete and Athens. But it was one of his little Abyssinian girls, bought in the slave market in Cairo, who really captured his heart. Satin-skinned, almond-eyed, gentle and sweet in temperament, Macbuba was one of the real loves of his life.

Returning home, he brought her with him. Lucie, waiting to greet the returning wanderer with open arms, was appalled to learn of his proposed addition to the household. She refused to welcome the girl, so Pückler made her comfortable in a pension in Vienna and visited her every day.

But Macbuba was dying. She succumbed to the harshness of the northern climate and tuberculosis ravaged her lungs. Pückler was grief-stricken and when she died gave her a sumptuous funeral at Muskau.

He continued to amuse himself with beautiful women.

There was Metternich's wife, Melanie, who made a fuss of him in Vienna, his old love Helmine's daughter, Lucie, who charmed him with her youth and freshness, and a countess who wrote him gushing letters. Then, when he was 60, came the pretty Countess de Rochfoucauld, whose ungrammatical screeds, devoid of a single comma, were stained with tears.

In 1845 he sold Muskau. Lucie, who loved the place, was furious. But Pückler felt as though a great burden had been lifted from his shoulders.

Now he devoted himself to his smaller estate at Branitz. The long-suffering Lucie grew difficult and egocentric with the years, and she and Pückler drifted apart. But he invited her to live at Branitz and it was there she died in 1854. When she had gone, the prince was lonelier than he ever realized he could be.

Strangely, his power over women seemed to increase with age. He remained extraordinarily young in appearance and at 80 had a serious affair with a Hungarian singer who prided herself on being a 'child of nature'.

Three years later he was on terms of warmest intimacy with the writer

Ludmilla Assing, who wrote to the 83-year-old Prince: 'My whole being melts away in the beauty and glory of yours. My heart is burning to ashes. I should like to enfold you like a creeping plant and in this most intimate embrace ask you for all your secrets.' He was still telling her he loved her 'fiercely' when he was 85.

He had gradually turned Branitz into another demi-Eden of trees, lakes, waterfalls and forests. Visitors said it was like something out of a fairy tale. Standing eerily on an island in a lake of cool, lapping water was his nostalgic gesture to his love of the East – a pyramid 60 feet high. Pückler would gaze at it for hours, sitting under a parasol with a fez on his head and a dwarf in attendance by his side.

Nobody thought of Pückler as old. He had volunteered for active service when war broke out between Prussia and Austria in 1866 and, though 81, was attached to headquarters staff. When France declared war on Prussia in 1870, he volunteered again, only to be told gently but firmly that he was too old.

At last even he had to accept that 'Prince Pickle' was no more. His spirits sank, his strength rapidly declined and on February 4, 1871, after a brief illness, he died at his beloved Branitz.

They buried him in the pyramid in the middle of the lake; then, sorting through his papers, they came across the extraordinary letters which told of a lifetime of mad, passionate, glorious, endless love . . .

Scourge – and pride – of Venice

Lover extraordinary who almost wed his own daughter

In his memoirs Casanova wrote: 'I felt myself born for the fair sex . . .' No one knows exactly how many women the immortal Italian lover seduced, but it was thought to be hundreds. His amorous career started at the age of 16 when he made love to two sisters in the same bed. It progressed through an extraordinary variety of amours including nuns, novices, duchesses, whores, lusty peasants and rich old ladies. He was able to fall madly and passionately in love within 15 minutes and no woman he desired had to wait more than a few seconds for the first move in the game. 'I have loved women even to madness,' he wrote.

But Casanova loved his freedom as much as he loved his women, and though several times he became entangled enough to be within sight of the altar, at the last minute he always escaped. He did it with the greatest subtlety, employing the most ingenious delaying tactics, until the bride-to-be got tired of waiting. When she inevitably made off with someone else he would retire to his bed for a couple of days, grief-stricken, before looking for consolation.

His opening move in an affair was often to provoke a quarrel or argument. He could then apologize, comfort and caress the offended beauty. He firmly believed that celibacy could ruin a healthy man's constitution. His own physique was strong and he had an enormous appetite for rich foods. Often, his seductions were carried out as part of a luscious feast. Crayfish or crab soup was a favourite starter followed by aphrodisiac oysters, which he slid between the breasts of his paramour and ate delicately in situ.

He did, at times, have moments of remorse for his libertine ways and would then consider going into a monastery – but a new beauty always arrived on the scene just in time to save him from his better self.

When his memoirs were first published – and they appeared in many different versions before the manuscript was at last printed exactly as Casanova had written it, in 1960 – they were received with disbelief. No man had ever left such an intimate record of his life. Some people questioned not only their authenticity but whether in fact such a man as Casanova ever really existed.

Contemporary portraits are not impressive, though he was said in his youth to have been exceptionally handsome. He was tall for an 18th-century Italian – 6 ft 1½ ins – with a fine head of hair and only three small pox scars to blemish his swarthy, acquiline profile. His fascination probably lay in his enormous stamina and energy, his commanding presence and air of virility. For Casanova was not just a profligate. He was one of the most brilliant figures of his age. Whatever he did, as lover, scholar, gambler, bon viveur, spy or raconteur, he did with colossal flair and charm.

He was born in Venice on April 2, 1725, the son of an actor and actress, in a city given over to sensuality. His parents neglected him and he was a miserable, sickly child whose nose was always bleeding. At the age of 9 he was taken to Padua to be educated. He lodged with the Abbé Gozzi, who taught him to play the violin, and he studied at Padua University until he was 16. Astonishingly, he became a priest himself – it was the most common thing for a man with talent but no money in those days. Yet Holy Orders did not stop him from 'losing his innocence' to two sisters, Nanette and Marton Savorgnan, daughters of a noble Venetian family. He spent the night with the pair of them in the same bed! From then on, he had a penchant for double seductions.

Having left the priesthood, Casanova entered on a life in which he lived largely by his wits. He was taken into the service of distinguished men, talked his way into the most brilliant society and, through letters of recommendation, moved up the social scale. The Prince de Ligne said he was 'one of the most interesting, odd characters' he had ever met. By the age of 20 he was also completely obsessed by gambling. He would stake his money on any game but Faro was then the rage of Europe and he became a past master. He thought nothing of gambling all night, all day and the next night without a break.

Every woman he desired he pursued with almost comic fervour. Visiting the estate of the wealthy Countess Mont-Real he was attracted by a newly married young woman of exceptional beauty and made advances to her – without success – whenever her husband turned his back. One afternoon Casanova persuaded her to go out riding in a two-wheeled chaise. A terrible thunderstorm frightened her almost to hysteria. 'Using a method of distraction which provided excitement closer at hand, I succeeded in curing her of her dread of thunder,' he wrote, 'although I doubted that she would reveal the secret of my remedy!' Between seductions of a similar nature Casanova went to sacred concerts and wrote Italian verses for church music.

His financial situation fluctuated wildly. At one time he was reduced to playing the violin in a theatre in order to keep himself. His only regular income was from patrons like the noble Venetian, Matteo Bragadin, former Inquisitor of State, who adopted him as a son and gave him a monthly allowance which he received until his protector's death.

However, he had an attitude of contemptuous insolence towards the ruling class in Venice that made him hated by the Establishment. He was even suspected of being a spy. His jealous enemies were ready to seize on anything to get him out of the way and eventually it was a religious satire he had written as a youth that gave them an excuse. On the night of July 25, 1755, he was arrested and taken to The Leads, the infamous Venetian prison, which derived its name from the heavy lead tiles that covered the roof. He was condemned to five years without trial. Perhaps, it was suggested afterwards, the fact that Casanova was wooing the mistress of one of the Inquisitors had something to do with it.

His escape from The Leads 15 months later was one of the classic prison breaks of history. He had managed to get hold of a piece of iron and patiently whittled it away with a fragment of marble until it was an 18-inch spike. He had made a gaping hole in the floor of his cell and was ready to put his escape plan into action when he was suddenly moved to more spacious accommodation in The Leads. The furious jailer threatened to report him to the authorities, but Casanova managed to keep him quiet. For his next attempt he enlisted the help of a fellow prisoner, a priest called Balbi. One day he called the jailer and asked him to take Balbi a huge Bible as a present. The Bible was to be delivered along with a plate of macaroni which Casanova recommended as being especially delicious. The Bible was placed on top of the macaroni and the jailer was too busy trying not to spill it to notice that the plate was extremely heavy. Casanova had slipped his iron spike into the Bible's parchment cover.

The priest, whose cell was above, bored a hole through Casanova's ceiling and hauled him through. Together the two men then drilled through to the great attic where they were usually taken to exercise, and from there it was easy enough to prise one of the lead sheets away from the roof. They scrambled out – and were away. Casanova hailed a gondola and spent the night in the home of the Chief of Gendarmes, who was out looking for him!

Casanova spent the next part of his life keeping out of the hands of the Venetian Inquisitors. His conquests consoled him. In Constantinople, however, he met with rare defeat. Despite the religious code which demanded the absolute division of the sexes, he had managed to mesmerize a Moslem lady he referred to as 'The Wife of Yussef'. One night he attempted to remove her veil and made her so angry he could do nothing but beat a hasty retreat. Afterwards he realized with chagrin that he had made a foolish mistake and that she would have been willing to take off everything else.

In Paris he was admitted to the most exclusive circles and was appointed a director of the French lottery. His interest in the occult and black magic fascinated certain women of high rank, among them the Marquise d'Urfé. He was her lover, of course, and she supported him lavishly for years but the poor woman, besides being rich, was also incredibly gullible. She was a Cabalist, a believer in a complicated pseudo-religious sect and reincarnation. She was certain that Casanova could communicate with spirits and asked him to transmigrate her soul into the body of a male infant. Casanova set about to oblige by making love to a carefully chosen virgin. If they could produce a son, he assured her, it would be the reincarnation of the Marquise. The mumbo jumbo went on for ages and was the scandal of Paris until Casanova tired of it. While he did not take advantage of the credulous old lady directly, he knew very well that he had power over her and relished it.

To keep up the dazzling life he was leading, however, he needed ever more

Portrait of Casanova aged 49

funds. He decided to go into business. In Paris there was a great vogue for painting patterns on silk after the Chinese fashion. This seemed an elegant enterprise to suit his tastes and he set up an establishment. He engaged 20 girls for the work, interviewing each one himself, to make sure she was attractive. Each girl in turn became his mistress. But while his love life flourished, his business did not.

As a lavish spender and gambler he was often at a loss for money and to obtain cash he would sometimes pawn his jewels and gold snuff boxes. He spent a fortune on women, anticipating their every whim and showering them with presents of jewels and clothes.

He usually came out of his affairs unscathed, but one encounter in Italy he was never to forget. Visiting the Duke de Matalone in Naples, he was introduced to the Duke's beautiful young mistress, Leonilda. He fell desperately in love with her, so much so that he asked the Duke to grant him her hand in marriage. The Duke affably agreed, amused to see Casanova so truly smitten. All that remained was to send for the girl's mother to put her name to the marriage contract. On the day she was expected to arrive, Casanova went out to deal with some business, returning to the ducal palace in time for supper. Waiting for him in the drawing room he found the Duke, Leonilda and Leonilda's mother, all in a state of happy excitement. When the latter saw Casanova she screamed and fainted. It was one of his old loves, Anna Maria Vallati, who had borne his child 17 years before. There was no doubt about it. He had been about to marry his own daughter.

Overcome with remorse, he offered to make amends and marry his old love instead, but Donna Lucrezia, as he used to call her, knew his character too well, and declined. After making Leonilda a handsome present for her eventual marriage, he set off again on his travels.

Casanova lived in England for nine months. He had been sent to try to set up the French form of lottery. While in London he was introduced to the famous courtesan, Kitty Fisher. He declined to take advantage of her favours for the simple reason that he did not speak English and therefore could not hold a conversation with her. Delicately, he explained that when making love the enjoyment of *all* his senses was necessary.

He played whist with English aristocrats and joined in the gay social life, but at his apartment in Pall Mall he languished alone. Piqued by this unusual solitude, he advertised some of his rooms to let, furnished, and netted a pretty, refined young Portuguese girl who spoke French and kept him company until her boat sailed for Lisbon.

But it was also in England that he had an experience from which he swore he could date his decline. He became involved with a shrewd little prostitute named Marianne Charpillon. To his rage and humiliation, she cost him 2,000 guineas and refused to grant him her favours. When she explained that she was dying of an incurable disease he was so distraught that he went 'laden with lead' to commit suicide in the Thames. Friends stopped him, telling him she was in fact, at that moment, merrily dancing the minuet. As a revenge he bought a parrot and taught it to repeat in French 'Charpillon is a greater whore than her mother'.

Casanova fled from England to avoid debts and returned to Venice in 1772 after years of exile. He was welcomed with open arms and even invited to dinner by the Inquisitors who were dying to know how he had in fact escaped from The Leads.

But as J. Rives Childs writes in his biography of Casanova: 'For him, as for Byron, the days of his youth were the days of his glory. He had drunk life to the lees as few men before him or after. ...' Now his glitter began to fade. He found he could not earn a living by his pen. His translation of the *Iliad*, though admired, had to be abandoned for lack of funds. In 1776, under the name of Antonio Pratolini, he became a secret agent for the Inquisitors. But the work did not suit his temperament. For a time he lived a quaintly domestic life in a small rented house with a little seamstress called Francesca Buschini, who was very sympathetic and devoted to him. However, he could never keep out of trouble for long and yet another affair of honour, a threatened duel and bitter words drove him from his birthplace once more and for the last time.

Some time in February 1784 Casanova met the Count Joseph Charles de Waldstein, whose great castle in Bohemia had a library of 40,000 volumes. They shared a love of gambling and the occult and after some persuasion he agreed to become the count's librarian. For the next 13 years, the last years of his life, he was bored to death. Only one thing interested him – the past. He spent hour after hour drafting and redrafting his memoirs, revelling in his moments of glory, savouring again the conquests of his youth. He held nothing back. Little did he realize that the account of his outrageous amorous adventures, translated into some 20 different languages, would one day be hailed as a literary masterpiece.

The outrageous Mrs Satan

She gave stock-market tips to Vanderbilt, lived with two husbands under the same roof and ran for the Presidency

As the model of a gracious, if slightly imperious, lady of the manor, nobody could beat Mrs John Biddulph Martin, whose banker husband, when he died, had left her Bredon's Norton in Worcestershire. She opened flower shops, turned her tithe barn into a village hall, took a proper interest in the education of local children and entertained the Prince of Wales, who sent her a basket of grouse.

Who could have guessed that this grande dame with the fine profile had once been dubbed 'Mrs Satan' for her outspoken ideas on free love, and had taken the extraordinary step of suing the British Museum when she realized that two documents on its shelves would shatter her new image?

Indeed, Mrs John Biddulph Martin was once considered the most outrageous woman in America, an eccentric who kept all her lovers under one roof and then had the nerve to put her name forward as a Presidential candidate. She was a visionary who claimed that Demosthenes, the ancient Greek orator, had guided her life, a fervent suffragette who told women to enjoy their sex life and take as many lovers as they wanted, a medium who gave spirit-world advice on stocks and shares to Vanderbilt himself. As a beautiful woman conducting a personal revolt against convention, Mrs Biddulph Martin, formerly Victoria Woodhull, shocked America for a decade.

She was fond of describing her birthplace as a picturesque cottage, painted white with a porch running round it and a garden in front. In fact, Victoria Woodhull was born on September 23, 1838, in a broken-down old shack full of noisy, brawling children out in the dusty frontier town of Homer, Ohio. Her father, Buck Claflin, ran a grist mill. Her mother, Roxanna, told fortunes and doctored her 10 children by hypnotism. Victoria started talking to spirits when she was three and said that her only friends in childhood were angels. Now and then she saw the devil.

One hot summer night the Claflin mill burned down in suspicious circumstances and Victoria's father, suspected of arson, was asked to leave town. The neighbours raised a subscription fund to send his family after him. For years the whole tribe wandered from town to town selling patent medicines and a complexion oil they concocted from vegetable juices. But it was when Victoria's youngest sister, Tennessee, announced that she too heard spirit voices, that Buck Claflin thought of a marvellous idea for making money. He set both girls to work holding seances. People at the boarding houses where they stayed often complained about the shrieks and weird noises. But the money rolled in. Victoria and her sister had found a career.

Victoria's wide blue eyes and rose-petal skin attracted men wherever she went. Before she was 16, she was married. Her husband was a young doctor called Canning Woodhull who mistakenly thought he was going to settle down. She bore him two children, a boy called Byron and a girl bizarrely named Zulu Maud, then decided Ohio was too small for her. She persuaded him to give up his practice and take her to California; then, missing her family, they moved on to join her sister, Tennie, in Cincinnati, where the two

Victoria Woodhull nominated for President of the United States

girls advertised themselves as clairvoyants. They usually gave rather noisy seances at a dollar a head. When they added fortune telling and magnetic healing the customers piled in – especially the men.

Poor Woodhull had not realized that marrying Victoria meant marrying the whole Claflin tribe. Soon he gave up the struggle and became a drunkard and a woman-chaser.

Victoria looked to Demosthenes for her next move. Apparently he turned up every now and then in a snow-white toga, pointing her in the right direction and consoling her with the promise that one day she would be wealthy.

Moving on to St Louis, she fell dramatically in love with a handsome young man sporting side whiskers, who called to seek her advice as a spiritualist. As soon as she saw him she wanted him. Her method was unique. She went into a trance, crying out that their destinies were linked. They were to be joined in marriage. The fact that both the caller, Colonel James Harvey Blood and Victoria herself were already married did not come into it at all. She told him they had been betrothed 'by the powers of the air'. Blood, an upstanding man and city auditor, looked into Victoria's blue eyes and succumbed. He left his wife and children and went off with her in a wagon.

After their spiritual betrothal they lived together as lovers; their house became a meeting place for radical thinkers and Victoria took to the lecture platform to practise what she preached.

But Demosthenes had promised her wealth and presumably it was he who led her to Cornelius Vanderbilt, the richest man in America. Vanderbilt was an ailing man and had lost patience with orthodox medicine. When Victoria and her sister were introduced to him as miracle healers from the West, he decided to give them a chance. The fact that they were both very attractive women probably had something to do with it. Victoria became his good friend – Tennie became his mistress.

Sometimes Vanderbilt asked Victoria for advice about the stock market from the spirit world, but he soon realized that his own instincts were better than advice from 'beyond'. Instead *he* gave *her* tips about stocks and shares. Victoria and her sister opened a brokerage office, the first to be run by women in the history of Wall Street, at the start of 1870. Business flourished, with Colonel Blood in the back office doing most of the actual work, and Victoria was able to fulfil her ambition; she rented a mansion and filled it with little gold chairs, gilt mirrors and servants!

Not three months after the sisters had astonished New York with their appearance in Wall Street, Victoria dropped the biggest bombshell of all. She announced herself as a candidate for the Presidency. With her suffragette hackles rising, she said she had proved herself in business to be the equal of men, so she reckoned she could act for the unfranchised women of the country. To promote her campaign she spoke on lecture platforms all over the country and launched a newspaper called *Woodhull and Claflin's Weekly* in which she lashed out at everybody who didn't agree with her and wrote articles supporting free love, abortion, birth control, legalized prostitution, vegetarianism, magnetic healing and easier divorce laws. It was a runaway success and achieved national distribution. Everybody wanted to hear what that dreadful Woodhull woman was saying.

Her household arrangements were, as usual, chaotic; full of over-ripe loves and hates. She had obtained a divorce and married Colonel Blood; then, to her horror, her first husband turned up on her doorstep, a pathetic wreck, ruined by drink and morphine. He had nowhere to go, so she took him in. Her mother, who hated Blood and was insanely jealous, chose this moment to bring a court case, swearing that Blood had assaulted her, and revealing that her daughter now had two husbands under one roof, if not in the same bed.

The press had a field day speculating on the love life of the Presidential candidate. But they didn't know half. Just about this time, Stephen Pearl Andrews appeared on the scene. He was the great intellectual in her life who knew 30 languages and had written a book in Chinese. He, too, joined the household. Then there was Theodore Tilton. 'He slept every night for three months in my arms,' she told the world. Whatever Colonel Blood *thought*, he made no complaints.

Tilton was one of the figures in a huge scandal that rocked America and put Victoria Woodhull behind bars. His wife had been seduced by the Rev. Henry Ward Beecher, the most famous preacher in America, believed by everyone to be the nearest thing to a saint. In fact, between sermons, Beecher had been making love to every pretty parishioner he could lay his hands on. Victoria was incensed that her honesty about free love had condemned her as a wicked woman, while Beecher was protected by a wall of hypocrisy.

She tried to force him into the open, met him, and even, so she claimed later, slept with him. But when she tried to blackmail him into supporting her on a public platform, he burst into tears and begged to be let off the hook.

What turned out to be her most famous appearance in public was booked at the Steinway Hall. Beecher had refused to introduce her as promised, and she went on stage in a fine passion.

'My judges preach against free love openly, and practice it secretly,' she stormed.

'Are you a free lover?' someone shouted.

'Yes,' she cried. 'Yes, I am a free lover.'

The audience burst into an uproar of cheers, hisses, boos and catcalls, but Victoria swept on, her voice rising above the din: 'I have an inalienable, constitutional and natural right to love whom I may, to love for as long or as short a period as I can, to change that love every day if I please! And with that right neither you nor any law you can frame have any right to interfere!'

Bedlam followed and was fully reported next day. The 'Free Love' speech, combined with her violent reactions and almost unprintable answers to questions, proved too much. She was asked to leave the splendid mansion she rented and spent a night on the pavement before she could persuade a boarding house keeper to take her family in. The brokerage business suffered, advertising disappeared from their newspaper and Vanderbilt gently withdrew his support. The suffragettes stood staunchly by her.

It was too unfair. Victoria decided it was time the whole truth was known about the Beecher-Tilton scandal. First of all she was seized by 'a great gust of inspiration' and told all she knew to an audience of spiritualists. Then she and her sister, Tennie, brought out a special edition of *Woodhull and Claflin's Weekly* on November 2, 1872, revealing the whole story. It was a sensation. Primly dressed in dark blue suits, they were both arrested for having circulated 'an obscene and indecent publication' and thrown into jail. They spent six months behind bars before a technical point gained them a verdict of 'Not Guilty'. The Beecher scandal dragged on for years. To some he remained a hero. Others branded him 'a dunghill covered with flowers'. His reputation never recovered.

The scandal did little to help Victoria in her bid for the Presidency. When Grant swept into office, she received only a few popular votes. Her private life, too, was in turmoil. Though she herself was having an affair with a 19-year-old college boy who helped to manage her lecture tours, she was furious to discover that Colonel Blood had also been seeking consolation. Outraged by his infidelity, she asked him to leave!

With his departure her fiery enthusiasm somehow seemed to wane. She took to religion. Then in 1877 Vanderbilt died and Victoria made it known that the old man owed her 100,000 dollars. His heir took the hint. He paid up with the proviso that both Victoria and Tennessee removed themselves from American soil until the business of the will was settled. With a new wardrobe, servants and six first-class state rooms, the sisters sailed for England.

Victoria decided to become a new woman. She had divorced Blood for infidelity. It was the first time that most people realized they had ever been legally married, for she had never taken his name. Free love was obviously on the scrap heap and when she lectured in England – she could never keep off a public platform for long – she chose subjects such as the sanctity of marriage and 'The Human Body, the Temple of God'.

Sitting in the audience at one of these lectures was a charming, highly respectable banker, John Biddulph Martin. He was a partner in Martin's Bank, the family firm, and 36 years old. Charmed by Victoria's 'high intellect' and fascinated by her personality, he determined to make her his wife. Martin's parents were appalled by his choice. They had read all about Victoria in the newspapers. So, the one-time free lover, certain that Demosthenes had led her to her destiny, set about to obliterate her past and present herself as a noble and much wronged woman. After six years they gave in and Victoria became Mrs John Biddulph Martin on October 31, 1883. She was 45 and proved herself, as to the manner born, perfect mistress of her husband's dignified mansion in Hyde Park Gate, London. For the next 18 years they lived happily together, the respectable banker thoroughly enjoying his extraordinary wife's company.

She never quite lived down her eccentric past and spent the rest of her life denying the outrageous things she was supposed to have said and done. Two documents on the shelves of the British Museum Library nearly gave her a heart attack. They were pamphlets on the Beecher-Tilton scandal, with ample reference to the part she played in it. She begged her husband to act, and the trustees of the British Museum were astounded to find themselves sued for libel. The trial, without precedent, lasted for five days and Victoria listened to it all with the air of a martyr, answering questions with such charming evasion that nobody quite understood what all the fuss was about. In the end the jury decided libel had been committed, but with no attempt to injure, and awarded her £1 damages!

When John Biddulph Martin died of pneumonia in 1879, Victoria sold her Hyde Park Gate house and moved into her husband's country manor at Bredon's Norton, there to live the life of a respected dowager of the English shires. Tennessee had also done well for herself. She became the wife of Sir Francis Cook.

But the old Victoria would not quite lie down. At the age of 63 she suddenly got bored with being respectable. She gave part of her estate for emancipated young women to learn farming, opened a school for progressive education, took up her old passion for spiritualism and involved herself in dozens of other things.

In her old age she refused to go to bed, always sleeping in a chair because she thought she could cheat death that way. For four years she slept upright, but on the morning of June 9, 1927, she was found to have drifted off in her sleep. One can't help hoping that it was Demosthenes who came for her.

His watery Lordship

How to be healthy and amphibious

Had Lord Rokeby been given the option, he would no doubt have preferred to have been born a frog. As it was, he did everything he could to turn himself into an amphibian. Convinced that water was his natural habitat, he stayed immersed for as much of his life as was humanly possible and became the watery wonder of 18th-century England.

He started life in a perfectly normal fashion as plain Mr Matthew Robinson, a member of a respectable and down-to-earth Scottish family who had moved south from Struan and settled in Kent. His father, Sir Septimus Robinson, distinguished himself by being made gentleman usher to King George II.

As heir to the family fortunes, he was given an excellent education and became a Fellow of Trinity College, Cambridge. People were somewhat surprised when he took up politics as an ardent Whig and joined the 'patriots' who called William of Orange to the English throne in order to ensure the Protestant succession. But in every other way he seemed the epitome of the cultured, affluent country gentleman.

In 1754, on the death of his courtier father, the family estate at Mount Morris, near Canterbury, passed into his hands and he devoted himself to the task of farming its wide acres, replacing its deer with black cattle and cultivating the land. He was so much admired for his shrewd good sense and engaging manner that he was chosen to represent Canterbury in parliament. He succeeded to the Rokeby title on the death of his uncle, Richard Robinson, Bishop of Armagh and Primate of Ireland.

Then, one fatal summer, Lord Rokeby decided to spend a holiday in the spa town of Aix-la-Chapelle. He 'took the waters' and blissfully submerged himself in the health-giving baths. It was a revelation! His career as an amphibian had begun.

Home in Kent, he began to make daily trips to the sea to immerse himself in salt water. As time went by it became increasingly difficult to persuade him to come out. He was convinced that water was good for his intestines and, besides, he never felt happier than when bobbing about in the waves.

As though his behaviour was not odd enough, he also took to growing a beard – not the normal sort of affair, but a great wild, woolly appendage which grew until it reached his waist and was so thick it stuck out under his arms and could be seen from behind.

Still an excellent host, he received many visitors who were consumed by curiosity to get a close view of the beard and to learn more about his addiction to water. Only one thing put them off. He had a passion for reading boring poems of enormous length to any captive audience.

He built himself a little hut on the sands at Hythe, about three miles from Mount Morris, and would launch himself into the sea, in all weathers, sometimes bobbing about for so long that he fainted and had to be carried from the water.

The daily procession which set out from Mount Morris to the beach was extremely bizarre. Lord Rokeby walked all the way, very slowly, with his hat tucked underneath his arm. His short, curiously curved figure was half-covered by his extraordinary bush of a beard. His clothes were as plain as those of his poorest tenant. But he insisted on being followed by his carriage and a favourite servant dressed in splendid livery. If it rained, Lord Rokeby made the servant ride in the carriage 'as he might spoil his clothes and catch the devil of a cold'. But his lordship carried on walking.

All along the route to the beach he had built drinking fountains so that his favourite liquid could be close to hand. He kept a number of half-crowns in his pocket and if he came across anyone drinking at a fountain as he passed by he would present them with a coin, together with a homily on the joy of pure water.

After a few years he grew weary of trailing all the way to the beach and decided to build a swimming-pool in the grounds of his mansion. It was under glass and heated by the sun.

Everyone was curious to see Lord Rokeby in his element, but few people managed it. He conducted the whole business with great secrecy and spent the greater part of his day alone in the water. However, there is one eye-witness account by an unnamed gentleman who had 'resolved to procure a sight of this extraordinary character', and it is reproduced in a fascinating book called *Public Characters*, printed in 1799. He describes how, after the necessary inquiries, he was conducted by a servant to a little grove at Mount Morris, in the middle of which was a building constructed of glass.

'The man who accompanied me opened a little wicket and, on looking in, I perceived immediately under the glass, a bath, with a current of water supplied from a pond behind. We then proceeded and, gently passing along a wooden floor saw his lordship stretched on his face at the farther end. He had just come out of the water and was dressed in an old blue woollen coat and pantaloons of the same colour. The upper part of his head was bald, but the hairs of his chin, which could not be concealed, even by the posture he had assumed, made its appearance between his arms on each side. I immediately retired and waited at a little distance until he awoke, when, rising, he opened the door, darted through the thicket, accompanied by his dogs, and made directly for the house ...'

As his habits became more and more solitary, all kinds of rumours began to circulate about him, one being that he was a cannibal and lived on raw flesh. In fact, his diet was extremely frugal and consisted mainly of beef tea. The cannibal rumour probably sprang from the fact that occasionally he would take a leg of roast veal with him into the water and take a nibble whenever he felt faint from hunger.

On rare occasions, he came out of the water to entertain a special guest. Prince William of Gloucester, travelling through Kent, had expressed a desire to meet him. He was evidently staggered by the luxurious dinner provided by this strange man. The food was magnificent, the choice of wines memorable and the Prince's dessert, it was reported, was accompanied by a fine Tokay that had been maturing in the cellars at Mount Morris for 50 years. Lord Rokeby himself would touch nothing but water. On even rarer occasions, he would take his best clothes out of mothballs and present himself at court. His sister, Mrs Elizabeth Montagu, a sparkling socialite, was terribly embarrassed. After one such appearance she wrote to her husband: 'I am glad he has gone back to the country. He has made a most astonishing appearance at court. I wish the beefeaters had not let him past the door!'

His strange behaviour was a constant source of anxiety to his poor sister, who enjoyed a splendid social life and lived in terror that her inconvenient brother might 'exhibit his amphibious and carnivorous habits at Bath'. For, like most fashionable women, she relished the season at the famous Regency spa town as much as the season in London, and wailed: 'I shall never be able to stand the joke of a gentleman's bathing with a loin of veal floating at his elbows, all the Belles and Beaux of the Pump Room looking on and admiring.'

Rokeby paid not a scrap of attention to her. His beard grew wilder and wilder until it nearly reached his knees, and he became extremely obstinate in his ways. He hated fires and refused to have them in the house even in the bitterest weather. His windows were kept open throughout the year. He also hated doctors and refused to be treated by them. Once he fell into a fit and the nephew who was with him at the time became alarmed and insisted that he must call for medical attention. Rokeby gathered his wits together and threatened to disinherit the young man if he let a doctor through the door.

Going to church was another of his pet phobias. He said that God could best be worshipped at the natural altars he had provided for mankind – the earth, the sea and the sky. He also complained that clergymen were too

The amphibious Lord Rokeby

preoccupied with trivia and preached boring sermons, and he would have nothing to do with them.

When he was 83 he stayed at the Chequers Inn at Lenham so that he could vote in the general election of 1796. By now he presented such an astonishing sight that inhabitants from all the nearby villages came to see him. They came to the conclusion that such a strange-looking man could not be an English lord. They decided he must be a Turk.

Old age had not tamed him at all. He was regarded as something of a marvel. His great bush of a beard did not stop him pursuing pretty girls, as he had done in his youth, and he seemed to thrive despite his profound contempt for all 'practitioners of physic'.

When he died peacefully at Mount Morris in December 1800 in his 88th year, he was mourned by many. The only wonder was that he died in his bed – it was a miracle that he didn't drown.

The greatest happiness ...

Benign law-reformer who adored cats

So fond of his cat was Jeremy Bentham, the great English moralist and law reformer, that one day he sat it on his desk and gave it a knighthood. From then on the puss was known to everyone, including the most distinguished callers, as 'Sir John Langborn'. When sedate old age began to catch up with Bentham's pet, he raised the cat to the dignity of the church, addressing it in full as 'The Reverend Doctor Sir John Langborn'. When the animal died, it was buried with full honours in Bentham's garden.

One of the most fertile thinkers of the 18th century, Bentham once said that he loved everything that had four legs. He worked for years, in a callous age, to bring about legislation against cruelty to animals. Being equally fond of cats and mice presented something of a problem, but he managed to feed and care for them both.

His affection for humble things extended even to everyday household articles, and he had a name for most of them. His favourite walking stick was called 'Dapple' and the teapot he used every day was addressed as 'Dick'. He lived in a delightful house with a walled garden in London's Queen Square Place, now known as Queen Anne's Gate. He called it 'The Hermitage' and himself 'The Hermit'.

Over the years he became so wedded to his routine and domestic rituals that he would allow very few people to visit him, spending most of the day covering sheet after sheet of paper with the ideas that swept in a torrent through his brain. Nothing was allowed to disturb his regular routine. French writer Madame de Stael applied for an introduction, saying: 'Tell Bentham I will see nobody till I have seen him.' Bentham replied dryly: 'Sorry for that. For then she will never see anybody!'

He was a picturesque figure in old age, with his white hair flowing over the shoulders of a brown Quaker-cut coat, a broad-brimmed yellow straw hat on his head and embroidered carpet slippers on his feet. He was in fact one of the happiest old men who ever lived.

In 1820 he wrote: 'I am, at 72, for one reason and another, gayer than I was at 17. Venerable they call me – those who have never seen me. Those who *do* see me would as soon think of calling a kitten venerable.'

He played a strenuous game of badminton at 75 and at 78 declared he had never been stronger in his life. In her biography, Mary P. Mack says that, reversing the usual course of development, he was born old and grew young.

Bentham started life miserably as a timid, lonely, precocious child. He was born in Houndsditch, London, on February 15, 1748, the son of an attorney who had made a fortune by speculating in real estate. By the age of three he had taught himself to read. Before he was five he had earned himself the nickname 'Philosopher'.

His father, Jeremiah Bentham, a prim, severe and inordinately ambitious man, was overjoyed to find that he had spawned a prodigy and saw him as a future Lord Chancellor before the babe was out of the nursery.

Poor Jeremy was crammed with Greek and Latin, and every minute of his day was occupied with tutors of one kind or another.

Half afraid of his father, he allowed himself to be pushed towards a legal career when all he really wanted was to be a chemist. For the rest of his life, whenever he felt depressed, he sought comfort in the smelly mysteries of his own private chemistry laboratory.

At the tender age of 12, he was entered for Queen's College, Oxford, the youngest student in the history of the University. He was a nervous child among the older students and he hated it. Nevertheless, he took his Bachelor of Arts degree at 15, his Master's degree at 18 and immediately afterwards was accepted as a student in the Court of King's Bench, London.

But things were not to turn out quite as the ambitious Jeremiah had planned. His son never became Lord Chancellor. He never distinguished himself as a barrister – indeed, he never spoke in court except to say a few formal words.

Instead he became the greatest critic of the English law as it stood, dedicated himself wholly to its reform, and set out to create a new science of morals and legislation. His great work was to be in the field of jurisprudence and ethics.

He lived at a time when justice went to those who could pay for it, when men were given the death penalty for stealing a handful of turnips to feed their starving children and when the majority of executions were for crimes against property.

Bentham thundered at his contemporaries: 'Magna Carta says justice shall be denied to no man; justice shall be sold to no man. Denied it is to nine-tenths of the population – and to the remaining one-tenth it is sold at an unconscionable price.'

From 1766 to 1792 Bentham lived in damp, gloomy lawyer's rooms at Lincoln's Inn. At 20 he was almost like a monk, sitting alone hour after hour, never content until he had covered 15 folio pages a day with his thoughts on law, morals, politics, or indeed any issue of vital human interest.

His only recreation was to take long, rambling walks in the back streets of London, which he loved. But his sense of direction was so vague that he usually got lost and would be found wandering with only a book in his pocket.

During these years he discovered the principle of 'utility' – that the proper end of all human activity is the greatest happiness of the greatest number – and it is for 'utilitarianism' that he is best remembered today. He spoke in favour of a welfare state, sexual freedom for all, women's rights and a reformed law at a time when such matters were, to say the least, unfashionable.

In 1792 his father died, releasing him from his awful sense of guilt at having failed him, and leaving him a small fortune as well as the family house in Queen Square Place. And when Jeremiah died a new Bentham was born. It was then he took to wearing his yellow hat and bright slippers. He also installed a piano or organ in every room of the house so that music could always be heard.

He dreamed up amazing inventions. He had an idea for 'conversation tubes' to be laid like water-pipes between buildings. And he designed a 'frigadarium', an igloo-shaped ice-house for storing the fruits of his garden as well as 'bullocks hearts, calves hearts and liver, rabbits and chickens, sprats and smelts, oysters and salmon'.

Deeply interested in penal reform, he also drew up plans for a new kind of prison, which he called a 'panopticon'. It was based on the idea of a wheel, with the prison 'inspector' at the hub able to see everything going on by means of reflectors. Bentham devoted many years of his life and a great deal of money in attempts to get his panopticon scheme accepted, but to no avail.

Then he set out to invent a new language in which he could more precisely express his science of morals and legislation. Many people scoffed at his 'neologisms'. One of the more preposterous was 'Brithibernia' which he urged the government to use to replace the separate names of England, Scotland and Ireland. Fortunately, it was never taken seriously. But some of his verbal inventions are today an accepted part of the English language – 'international', for example, and words like 'codify' and 'maximize'.

The whole of his domestic life at Queen Square Place was geared to the strict routine that allowed him to complete his mandatory 15 folio pages of writing each day. He seldom saw anyone till seven o'clock dinner.

He revelled in rituals. Meals were served on the dot. After dinner, in all weathers, he took a 'post prandial circumgyration'. This was supposed to be a leisurely walk around his garden, though guests who were invited to join him usually found they had to break into a sharp trot in order to keep up with

An effigy of Jeremy Bentham with his mummified head below

him. He was the most delightful and gracious host but when the clock struck eleven, Bentham would call for his 'putter to bed' and even the most distinguished guest would know that it was time to leave.

The ritual of going to bed took precisely one hour. After he had undressed and tied on a nightcap, he would hand his watch solemnly to a secretary and request him to read aloud. Finally, he bade his cats goodnight and climbed into a sleeping sack of his own design.

Bentham never stopped writing. In addition to his daily folios, there were endless lists, catalogues and prefaces to books he would not even start.

Thoughts came to him so fast that he hardly had time to deal with them. Sometimes he would jot down an idea on a piece of paper and pin it to the curtains. Eventually all the hangings in his room were covered with fluttering scraps.

He wrote so much that he often forgot what he had written. He was extremely surprised one day to come across an analysis on parliamentary reform. 'What can this be?' he scrawled across the front of it. 'Surely this was never *my* opinion!'

The edition of Bentham's writings edited by Sir John Bowring runs to 11 volumes and still omits several full-scale works. Innumerable manuscript pages are packed away in dusty old tin trunks, still unread, because of the great difficulty of deciphering Bentham's handwriting.

In 1825 he decided to leave his 'Hermitage' for a short spell and went to Paris to consult a doctor about his health. While there he took the opportunity to attend a session at the Courts of Justice. As he entered, the whole Bar rose to its feet and the president insisted that the great English jurist should sit on his right hand. It was a moment that his late father would have given his chance of eternity to see.

Bentham continued to find his greatest happiness in work, even in the last years of his life, and his rituals were performed without interruption. Death came peacefully and aptly on June 6, 1832 – the day before the great Reform Bill received the Royal Assent.

But that was by no means the end of Jeremy Bentham. Shortly before his death he wrote that he thought the bodies of the illustrious should be preserved as a reminder of their achievements; that every man, if embalmed, could be his own statue.

He left his own body to the university to be dissected, as he wanted it to be of some use to humanity. The skeleton was then dressed in his old Quaker coat, the yellow straw hat placed on an effigy of his head, and 'Dapple', his favourite cane, laid across his knee.

Today, Jeremy Bentham still sits and gazes benignly at curious visitors from a glass case at University College, London.

The elusive billionaire

Solitary confinement in germ-free luxury hotels

In a small, darkened room at the top of the nine-storey Desert Inn, Las Vegas, Howard Hughes, the American billionaire, lay on his bed watching a film. His skinny frame was stark naked apart from a pair of drawstring underpants. His hair and beard hung to his waist in lank, greasy strands. Every now and then he would reach out a claw-like hand with 2-inch-long yellowed nails to buzz for someone to come and change the reel. Hughes had been in that room for three months on one of his incredible film-watching marathons and in all that time he ate nothing but candy bars and nuts washed down with glasses of milk. His favourite movies were all-action dramas and he had sat through *Ice Station Zebra* 150 times with the sound turned up so loud it bounced off the walls.

Many people were surprised that Howard Hughes was still alive in the 1960s, let alone watching films night and day. He had turned himself into one of the great mysteries of the 20th century. For 15 years the once-handsome man about town, who owned most of the casinos in Las Vegas and escorted beautiful women by the score, had shut out the world, living in dark rooms, guarded by men who seldom saw him.

Howard Hughes developed such a dread of coming into contact with people, such a horror of touching anything that other people had touched, that he turned evasion into a science and secrecy into a religion.

He was born rich in Houston, Texas, on Christmas Eve, 1905. His father owned an oil-drilling tool company and when he died he left it to Howard. The young tycoon was then in a position to gratify any fancy that took him. Hollywood was just beginning to catch fire and when he was 21 he decided to shake the dust of Texas off his feet and become part of the new, glamorous world of picture-making.

He became an independent producer and almost immediately made his mark on an industry that never failed to fascinate him. He produced *Scarface*, one of the classic gangster films of all time which made international stars of Paul Muni and George Raft, and *Hell's Angels*, the picture that introduced Jean Harlow to the screen.

Actresses found him hard to resist and Hollywood was littered with apartments he had bought for adoring stars and starlets. He made it perfectly clear that they could stay around as long as they pleased – but only if they reserved their favours for him alone. He soon forgot them. Jean Harlow was dated, given a fabulous apartment, then ignored. In the 1930s and 1940s he often had as many as 20 beautiful girls on his dating list. Film stars liked being seen with him and in his heyday he could take his pick, escorting beauties like Ava Gardner, Elizabeth Taylor, Lana Turner, Ginger Rogers, Mitzi Gaynor and Cyd Charisse.

Signs of his eccentricity came with his discovery of Jane Russell. He found her behind the reception desk when he went to have his teeth seen to, launched her in *The Outlaw* and began to take an obsessive interest in her bust. He wrote pages of notes to cameramen about how her bosom should appear on film and invented a special cantilevered bra to show her shape off to the best advantage.

But films were only part of the scene for Howard Hughes. He was a business tycoon on America's biggest scale and owned two aircraft companies: Trans World Airlines and Hughes Aircraft. He was crazy about planes and a keen pilot. During the Second World War he decided to do his bit for the war effort by building planes. The first was a monster called the 'Hercules' – an eight-engined flying boat weighing 200 tons, designed to carry 700 passengers. The plane's wingspan was slightly longer than a football pitch and its tail the height of an eight-storey building.

He put 50 million dollars into the project, but the plane only flew once. Hughes himself took it up and managed to keep it in the air for just one mile. The second plane was an experimental long-range reconnaissance design in which he had great faith. But on the first flight, with Hughes at the controls, it crashed. He sustained appalling injuries which left him in pain for the rest of his life and started his dependence on drugs.

Sometimes, tired of his lifestyle, he would disappear for six months. On one of these jaunts he piloted a private plane to Louisiana and was forced to land with engine trouble. He wandered into the nearest town and tried to hire a car to drive on to Florida. He had 1,200 dollars in his pocket but no identification, so the police were called and he was taken to the nearest jail as a vagrant. When he protested that he was Howard Hughes, the policeman looked him up and down and retorted: 'You're a bum.' No wonder. He was unshaven, wore a crumpled, dirty suit with gym shoes and carried sandwiches and a bottle of milk in a paper bag. He was not released until someone was found to identify him.

Hughes married twice. His first wife was Ella Rice; then in 1957 he wed film actress Jean Peters. She later told how she was treated almost like a prisoner in the Bel Air mansion which was their home. From the start, Hughes insisted that they not only had separate bedrooms but separate refrigerators and facilities for cooking. No one, he insisted, not even his wife, was allowed to touch his food. The marriage came to an end with a one million dollar settlement. Hughes, becoming more and more averse to human contact, retreated to a bungalow in the desert near Las Vegas and hired his famous 'Mormon Mafia', a group of men of Mormon faith whose sole job in life was to protect him from outside contamination.

One of the main reasons for his desperate efforts to isolate himself was a growing terror of germs. He told a newspaperman: 'Everybody carries germs around with them. I want to live longer than my parents, so I avoid germs.'

When visitors drove out to the desert they had to stand in a chalk square drawn on the paving outside to be inspected before they were allowed near his front door. Even his own doctor was only allowed to 'examine' him from the other side of the room. Beside his chair he kept a huge box of paper tissues. They were his life savers, his 'insulation' against the bug-ridden world. He would touch nothing without first covering his hand with a Kleenex.

But, however strange his behaviour in this respect, he remained the old Howard Hughes in business. He had a zest for tough negotiating and loved to hold secret meetings to discuss million-dollar deals.

Robert Gross of Lockheed had every reason to remember his meeting with him over the proposed sale of the Hughes Aircraft Company. Hughes insisted on driving Gross away from the bungalow into the desert so that they would not be overheard. They drove mile after mile in searing heat along roads that threw up clouds of dust. The car windows were firmly shut and Hughes insisted they stayed that way. When they stopped to talk he made Gross stuff handkerchiefs in all the air vents because he thought their conversation might be heard outside the car. The fact that there wasn't a living soul for miles and his companion was fainting from the heat didn't deter him. Once the car was hermetically sealed, he got down to business.

On one occasion, when Hughes discovered his room had been 'bugged', he immediately ordered 20 new Chevrolet cars. Puzzled aides asked him what on earth he was going to do with them all. For one thing, he said, he'd use a different one every day. 'No one will be able to bug 20 cars and no one will know which I am going to use.'

By the time he reached his mid-50s even the desert bungalow was not secluded enough for him. From now on he led a nomadic existence, wandering from one luxury hotel to another. Each time, the move was made with utter secrecy, the whole Hughes entourage scurrying out through kitchen exits and down fire-escapes before daybreak, carrying 'the boss' strapped to a stretcher.

Howard Hughes in his monoplane 'Winged Bullet'

At each luxury hotel he took the whole penthouse floor. Guards who were never allowed to see him were stationed outside the apartment while TV sets monitored 'dangerous' spots like lavatory windows and fire-escape doors. His aides and the 'Mormon Mafia' spread themselves out in the luxurious rooms while he sealed himself into the smallest he could find. Windows were darkened and taped, all furniture was removed apart from a bed and a chair. There were no books, pictures or personal touches about the room; only the film equipment with a screen at the end of the bed, and a huge box of paper tissues.

Nobody knew the truth about those years until after his death when James Phelan, an American investigative reporter who had been trying to break through the 'Secrecy Machine' for two decades was approached by aides Gordon Margulis and Melvin Stewart who had been with him right to the end, and at last he was given the whole incredible story.

They told how Hughes had reduced himself to a skeleton by an atrocious diet that depended entirely on whim – and their boss, they said, had a 'whim of steel'. Sometimes he would live on tinned chicken soup for weeks, eating it so slowly while he watched the screen that the same tin would have to be reheated over and over again. Sometimes he'd go for the candy bar, nuts and milk menu. For days he would eat nothing but ice-cream, sticking to one flavour until every ice-cream parlour in the district had run out of it.

Even when he consented to eat normally, he would order the same dinner day after day – steak, salad and peas. The peas were inspected carefully and all those over a certain size pushed to the side of the plate.

He refused point blank to have his hair or nails cut and only submitted twice in 10 years to a barber and manicurist. On those rare occasions he insisted that the barber wash and scrub up like a surgeon before being allowed anywhere near him. But the man could hardly complain; Hughes paid him 1,000 dollars for the haircut.

Only three times during 15 years in hiding did Howard Hughes consent to meet someone from the outside world. His hair was cut, his waist-length beard reduced to a smart Vandyke and his nails trimmed back and polished. But he insisted on leaving his left thumbnail about half an inch long and squared off. 'That's my screwdriver,' he explained. 'Don't trim my screwdriver too short.' He used it to flick over pages of business documents, tighten loose screws and make adjustments to his film equipment.

The only clothes he possessed were a dressing gown, a couple of pairs of pyjamas, a pair of sandals, an old-fashioned Stetson and a few pairs of specially made underpants or shorts, fastened with drawstrings. Sometimes he just refused to wear anything and sat stark naked with a napkin over his private parts.

It took an earthquake to force Howard Hughes out into the open. On the night of December 23, 1972, he was holed up in the usual fashion on the top floor of a hotel in Managua, capital of Nicaragua. Most people had gone to bed and everything was quiet when suddenly it started. The whole hotel shook and heaved, the world seemed to be full of screams and horrendous crashes. Melvin Stewart, the devout Mormon aide who had just said his prayers and gone to bed, managed to fight his way through the debris to Hughes's bedside and persuaded him to get dressed. 'He was the calmest man in Managua,' said Stewart afterwards.

They hustled him onto a stretcher and a little group managed to manhandle him through the wreckage to a Mercedes still in one piece in the parking lot. From there he was whisked out to a baseball field, away from the danger of falling buildings.

When the sun came up it was on a scene of utter chaos and destruction, with smoke and dust still rising from the rubble of one of the worst earthquakes of modern times. Hughes muttered something about sending funds to help rebuild the hospitals but otherwise seemed aloof from the hellish devastation around him and wanted to get back indoors. He was taken to President Somoza's house and pushed into a bathing cabin by the side of the swimming pool. The light, he complained, was hurting his eyes, and someone found a blanket to hang over the window.

An executive jet was sent for and he was flown to Florida, only to insist, within a few hours, on being taken to London. There he took refuge on the top floor of London's Inn on the Park. It looked as though the routine would be the same as anywhere else. But when news came through that after 12 years of bitter wrangling the US Supreme Court had cleared him of imposing self-serving deals on TWA, and had dismissed a 170-million-dollar judgment hanging over his head, he was in unusually high spirits.

His good humour was surprising enough, but nobody was prepared for his staggering announcement that he wanted to pilot a plane again. Everyone rushed about looking for something he could wear. Margulis was sent out for suits and shirts and the rest combed London for an old leather flying jacket and a snap-brim Stetson, the sort he wore in his great days as an ace pilot. He was not allowed to take the controls but went up as a co-pilot in a private jet and seemed to revel in the freedom.

It was short-lived. A few weeks later he fell and broke his leg in the bathroom. Though he had four doctors on his payroll and had given millions to medical research, he refused to take their advice and was never to walk again.

Yet he still insisted that after a brief stay at one hotel, the whole caravan must move on to another and the exhausting business of packing up, strapping his emaciated body onto a stretcher and spiriting him down fire-escapes continued.

Finally, in a darkened room at the Acapulco Hotel in Mexico they knew the end had come. While the rich, the young and the beautiful enjoyed the good life in the rest of the hotel, and superb brown bodies toasted in the sun, a doctor gazed with horror at the famous Howard Hughes. His body, wrecked with drugs and malnutrition, was down to 90 pounds in weight. His hair and beard had grown again almost to his waist and his nails were like eagle's talons.

Howard Hughes died on the plane taking him back home to Houston, Texas, in one last frantic bid to save him. The secret days were over.

A world of their own

The ladies of Llangollen built a Utopia

For 50 years Eleanor Butler and Sarah Ponsonby lived in a world of their own making. They seldom set foot outside it. Every minute of each day was planned and recorded. Everything was ordered, tasteful and beautiful.

Queens, princes and poets expressed delight in the little Eden which the two spinsters had created from a plain stone cottage and four acres of rough ground in the Welsh hills. In their later years, the two gentle old women looked for all the world like a pair of clergymen, with their cropped hair, dark riding habits, starched neckcloths and enormous, stout walking shoes.

Eleanor and Sarah were brought up in formal, aristocratic Irish families. They lived only a few miles from each other and their friendship probably began through a love of books.

It was in the spring of 1778 that they decided to run away together and shut out the world.

Eleanor, then a hefty 39-year-old, was regarded by her family as a handful and 'over-educated'. She spoke fluent French, read avidly and was bored and frustrated by life at Kilkenny Castle. Her mother had decided that the only future for her difficult daughter lay behind the walls of a convent.

Sarah, shy, sensitive and 16 years younger than Eleanor, lived with relations, Sir William Fownes and his wife Betty, at nearby Woodstock. But Sir William's roving eye was beginning to be a nuisance. Sarah grew increasingly upset by his attentions.

Secretly, she and Eleanor drew up a blueprint for a perfect life in what was then fashionably known as 'rural retreat'.

In April 1778 Lady Betty wrote an agitated letter to a friend: 'My dear Sally (as she called Sarah) lept out of a Window last Night and is gon off...' Sarah had, of course, 'gon off' with Eleanor.

But they were not allowed to escape so easily. They were hunted, found, brought back and subjected to all the wrath of outraged righteousness. Society of the day had no understanding of friendship between women and thought that marriage should be a woman's only ambition.

Finally, after a period of terrible emotional blackmail when they were urged again and again to give up their plans, they were allowed to go.

They intended to set up house together in England, but on a tour of Wales they found a simple white cottage, Plas Newydd, with a stone roof, in the rough hills behind Llangollen. They were able to rent it with four acres of land for the princely sum of £11 7s 6d per half year.

They began to live according to the system they had worked out in their unhappy days in Ireland, and vowed never to spend a night away from home so that their lives could progress smoothly, without interruption. In 50 years they seldom broke their pledge.

Their small fund of money was soon exhausted and they could rely only on about £280 yearly from unforgiving relatives. But on this small allowance they began a romantic overhaul of Plas Newydd, furnishing, decorating and renovating in Gothic style with stained glass windows, pointed arches and beautiful draperies.

They ran up enormous debts and Eleanor's accounts books over the years reveal constant financial crises. Only a few friends knew where they were and saved them by timely loans or gifts. But even in their worst times the two women managed to keep a gardener, a footman and two maids.

Slowly the cottage was changed from a simple dwelling into a retreat, set out in every detail with superb good taste and with a small but valuable library.

Their day was designed to be as perfect as they could make it, from the moment they rose early to walk in the garden and listen to the birds until the quiet evening hours when they played backgammon and read together, curling their hair in papers before the kitchen fire.

They devoted their whole lives to self-improvement, reading an astounding number of books each year, making their surroundings beautiful and ignoring what was then called 'polite society'. They would usually hide behind the curtains when they saw strangers walking down the path.

In the town of Llangollen they were known simply as 'The Ladies'.

Outside the cottage their four rough acres were gradually transformed into an exquisite miniature estate with shrubberies of syringa, white lilac, laburnum and wild cherry, gardens with asparagus beds and peach trees, and quiet paved walks lined with lavender and cabbage roses. They built a circular stone dairy which was a model of its kind, and their cow sheltered in a barn overhung with blossoms.

No detail was too small to be considered and not a minute of the day was wasted. They mastered Italian, did fine handwork, drew maps and lectured each other on literary subjects. Eleanor recorded their crowded days in her diary – even when she lay prostrate with migraine.

The only thing which they did not consider worth time and money was fashion. Their clothes were always years out of date and they even wore men's beaver hats because they withstood the weather better than bonnets.

After a few years, descriptions of their life together at Plas Newydd crept through to the outside world. They began to receive distinguished visitors. The young Duke of Wellington, then Sir Arthur Wellesley, called with his aunt. Robert Southey, the poet, stayed with them. William Wordsworth wrote poetry at their home.

Queen Charlotte of England was told of their 'perfect retirement' and asked to see a plan of the garden and cottage. They were overcome with joy when the King granted them a small pension.

Their devotion to each other lasted a lifetime. They shared everything. Their books and china bore both sets of initials. Their letters were signed jointly. They even insisted on using the royal 'we'.

Eventually both families came to accept their achievement and they were reconciled with them.

Eleanor Butler and Sarah Ponsonby died long years ago and today Plas Newydd stands an empty shell, much of its gardens overgrown or vanished. But more than one visitor in search of the past claims to have glimpsed their quiet ghosts.

The Ladies of Llangollen

SPORTING ODDS

The sporting world has always been crammed with
colourful characters. Some of them have found almost
superhuman energy to pursue their passionate
gamesmanship . . . like the squire who played billiards
non-stop for 50 hours – and the huntsman who
galloped around the countryside stark naked . . .

The biggest balloon of all

Earl's 20-year dream goes up in smoke

Ardent balloonist Benjamin O'Neill Stratford, sixth and last Earl of Aldborough, devoted his life and fortune to constructing what he intended to be the biggest balloon the world had ever seen.

Born in 1809 into a family that had already boasted eccentrics, he became a recluse and was seldom seen outside the walls of his family estate, Stratford Lodge, Baltinglass in Ireland. His entire life was given over to designing and building his giant dirigible.

His workshop, in the grounds of Stratford Lodge, was a vast hangar with doors 60 feet high and 50 feet wide, which had been built out of chiselled Wicklow granite. Inside, with the greatest secrecy, he worked for 20 years to bring his dream to reality.

During all that time he was waited on by only one servant. He refused to hire a cook and had his meals sent down to him from Dublin every day on the Blessington to Baltinglass Royal Mail coach. No one ever saw him out in company and he never travelled up to Dublin, went to parties or entertained. Nothing could distract him from his all-absorbing ambition: to see his great balloon rise into the air.

Once it was finished he planned to take it himself on its inaugural flight to England and from there he hoped to be able to cross the Channel to France. He had already purchased a plot of land on the banks of the Seine where he fully expected to be greeted by half the balloonists in Europe.

Aldborough's balloon was almost completed about the time of the Crimean War. Suddenly, with a rush of patriotism, he offered it to the British Army, explaining that with the addition of a platform, it could be used to ferry troops.

Then tragedy struck. One Sunday morning in 1856, Stratford Lodge went up in flames and sparks flew in all directions. Lord Aldborough apparently was not the least bit interested in the fate of his family seat. 'Save the balloon house,' he shouted to the local people who had flocked from Baltinglass to watch the blaze. Frantically he formed the onlookers into a human chain and hundreds of buckets of water were flung in the direction of the great hangar. But the flames and sparks were too fierce and before long the balloon itself went up in a sheet of flame.

Heartbroken by the catastrophe, Lord Aldborough felt he had nothing else to live for. For a time he moved into the ruins of the balloon house with a few pieces of furniture salvaged from the house. But he never recovered his spirits. Even if the will had been there, he could not have started all over again, for what was left of the family fortune had been spent on his first experiment.

He went to live at Alicante in Spain and helped to augment his income by breeding dogs and selling patent pills. But gradually he became more of a recluse than ever. Living in hotels, he would order his meals to be sent up to his room, but would not allow the dirty dishes and cutlery to be collected. When one room became full of litter and old crockery, he simply moved to another.

Strangely enough, that was not quite the end of his balloon. Peter Somerville, who tells Aldborough's story in his book on Irish eccentrics, says that back home in Ireland the Catholic Church at Baltinglass was reconstructed with some of the stone from the balloon house, and that for many years the fishing rods in the neighbourhood were made out of cane salvaged from the wreckage.

The streaking squire

A-hunting he would go . . . stark naked

Snow, ice and blizzard meant little to Shropshire squire John Mytton. Whatever the weather he would go shooting – often wearing only his birthday suit. Stark naked, he would chase startled wild duck across frozen lakes. Then he would trot home for his daily tipple of up to eight bottles of port or brandy.

'Jack' Mytton was one of the wildest characters ever to storm onto the English hunting scene. He lived for excitement and danger, revelling in escapades that would have been the death of most people.

His usual winter shooting gear, even in the bitterest weather, was a light jacket, linen trousers and the finest silk stockings. His boots were as thin as dancing shoes and he wore each pair out in two days. But even these flimsy clothes would be cast off in the thrill of the chase as he crashed through the ice of ponds and struggled through the mire of bogs.

Nothing stood in his way. When driving his gig he would tear across the quiet Shropshire countryside as if he were a Roman charioteer; he would laugh boisterously every time he escaped disaster.

Once he drove a gig at high speed into a rabbit hole to see if it would turn over. No one was in the least surprised when it did. Another time, he tried to jump his horse and carriage over a toll gate. He walked unscathed from the wreckage.

When Mytton the human disaster found a place to 'happen', friends were welcome to share the thrill. A companion who complained about Mytton's reckless driving evoked only a chuckle. Mytton asked his friend if he had ever been overturned in a gig.

'No, thank God,' answered his passenger.

'What a damned slow fellow you must have been all your life,' roared Mytton and promptly ran a wheel into the grassy bank so that the gig turned over.

Again Mytton escaped unhurt. So did his friend.

Born in 1796, Mytton came from a long line of Shropshire squires who sent their sons to parliament and were highly regarded by country society. When his father died he was left the family seat at Halston Hall, near Shrewsbury, £60,000 in cash and an income of about £10,000 a year. He squandered the fortune within 15 years.

When friends tried to warn him that his fortune was dwindling he ignored them. Bundles of notes were once found in the grounds of his estate, presumably dropped by Mytton. He never kept an account of the money he gave his servants to spend for him. And once at Doncaster races he lost several thousand pounds – his winnings – which blew away on the wind as he tried to count them.

His riotous behaviour was regarded as scandalous by sophisticated families in the neighbourhood, but working people on his estate loved his antics. When they saw him hurtling along the lanes they would cheer, for he was generous and contemptuous of the class distinctions of his age.

They also liked him because he was a fighter. Heavily muscled, he fought dogs and even bears when he was full of port and in want of exercise.

One day while Mytton was hunting, a troublesome Welsh miner tried to divert the squire's hounds. Mytton climbed from his horse and challenged the miner to a fight – under the 'gentlemen's rules' of the day. The two fought 20 rounds before the miner gave in. Then Mytton, admiring his opponent's courage, gave him half a sovereign and told him to get himself a hot meal.

John Mytton rides a bear into a dinner party

The wild squire loved to shock friends and laughed at their reactions to his pranks. He arrived at a dinner party in full hunting dress – riding a brown bear. He tried to make the bear go faster by digging in his spurs. The animal sank its teeth into the squire's calf. The prank ended in chaos and a doctor had to be called.

But Mytton was usually kind to his animals. His favourite hunter was Baronet, a game little one-eyed horse that had been his charger when he was in the Hussars, and which could clear a jump of nine yards over water. He had another horse that would rear in its shafts at a word of command until its haunches were almost touching the ground.

Though he cared little for his own comfort, he would sometimes knock at a cottage door during hard weather and ask if his horse could dry off by the fire. He gave another of his favourite horses, Sportsman, a bottle of port to keep out the cold. The horse drank thirstily. Soon afterwards it dropped dead.

By 1830 Mytton's friends were shaking their heads and saying among themselves that it was 'all up with Jack Mytton'. Constantly drunk, ravaged by the self-imposed harshness of his physical life and deeply in debt, he fled to France to avoid creditors.

He had, however, one more story to add to those that were endlessly repeated about him. One night he had hiccups. Recollecting that they could be cured by a shock, he set fire to his nightshirt. The hiccups stopped, but friends arrived only just in time to save him from serious burns.

He hated living abroad and yearned for the hunting fields of Shropshire. So in one last defiant gesture, he returned to England. The bailiffs were waiting.

In 1834 he died in a debtors' prison when only 38 years old, but his popularity lasted until the end. More than 3,000 friends and hunting companions attended his funeral.

The pint-sized athlete

He outstripped the first locomotive for a bet

Though he was only just over five feet tall, George Osbaldeston – known as 'The Squire of All England' – could never resist a challenge. He would go to the most extraordinary lengths to prove that he was the champion at anything, and 19th-century England gaped with amazement at his sporting triumphs.

His greatest feat, and the one that made him notorious, took place in 1831 when he declared he could ride a horse as fast (or nearly as fast) as Mr Stephenson's new-fangled *Rocket* locomotive, which travelled at an unprecedented 24 miles per hour.

Although at this time he was 44 years old and suffered from a badly crippled leg, injured years earlier in a hunting accident, he bet an old gambling crony, Colonel Charrite, 1,000 guineas that he would ride 200 miles in 10 hours.

For weeks nobody talked of anything else.

Bets were laid all over England, and Osbaldeston confidently backed himself for thousands of pounds in side bets. Then, a few days before the books were closed, he received a visit from the famous racehorse owner John Gully. Gully said he knew 'damn well' the squire could cover the distance in 10 hours. But, he urged, he would get even better odds if he did it in *nine*.

Osbaldeston scented greater glory, and, as Gully knew he would, took up the challenge with relish. He trained furiously, riding 80 miles a day, every day, in all weathers. He decided to cover the 200 miles, not along a stretch of road, but round and round the four-mile racecourse at Newmarket. He reckoned on doing it by using 28 horses, changing each time he completed a circuit and riding the liveliest animals several times over.

On the morning of the great race, Osbaldeston arrived at Newmarket in the early hours. It was pouring with rain and looked distinctly unpromising. The few spectators who had already gathered raised a cheer when they spotted his short muscular figure, resplendent in purple silk jacket, white breeches and black velvet cap. But before they could take in what was happening, he was up, off and away.

He rode like a mud-spattered fury while the whole sporting world waited, watches in hand. Climbing stiffly from the saddle at the end of the day, he found he had completed the course in eight hours and 42 minutes. He had averaged 26 miles per hour, allowing for stops, changes and a tussle with a bad-tempered horse called Ikey Solomon!

Once Osbaldeston knew the result, he flung himself back into the saddle and galloped off to the *Rutland Arms* in Newmarket where, after a steaming hot bath and a good rub down with oil, he announced he was so hungry he could 'eat an old woman'.

Within weeks he was throwing down the gauntlet again by offering to ride 200 miles in eight hours. But no one took him up. They had no doubt that if he set out to do it, he would.

George Osbaldeston was born on Boxing Day, 1787, educated at Eton and Oxford, but left University without bothering to take a degree because he could not wait to get on with the serious business of fox hunting. He started his career as Master of Hounds while still an undergraduate, purchasing a pack from the Earl of Jersey. Then, as a young man, he hunted all over Lincolnshire, Leicestershire and Northamptonshire, eventually becoming Master of the famous Pytchley Hunt.

He swore that any week in the hunting season that did not include six full days in the saddle was a waste of time. He exhausted his hounds and bought great mastiffs, hoping they would prove tougher. But even they couldn't keep up with him.

It was said that his knowledge of hounds was unrivalled. Certainly his strength and endurance and almost crazy determination were the marvel of the day. He once played billiards for 50 hours without a wink of sleep and, as the fastest bowler in English cricket, saved an important match by bowling dead drunk and with a broken shoulder.

His skill as a boxer, athlete and oarsman was equally exceptional and as a shot he was miraculous. One autumn day he brought down 100 pheasants with 100 shots. People were, therefore, all the more astonished when he spoke in a high-pitched, falsetto voice!

The 'Squire's' manners towards the 'lower orders' would often be rough and ready, especially when they interferred with his sport. But he often made up for it by ordering the local tavern to serve ale all around at his expense.

Sometimes he could show courtesy of a most sensitive kind. Once, at the Lincoln County Ball, he was introduced to a beautiful young lady called Miss Burton, who was later to become Lady Sutton. Osbaldeston was enchanted by her and watched her closely all night. He saw her go up to a rival 'belle' of the ball to compliment her on the posy of flowers she was carrying, in the centre of which was a very rare orchid. Miss Burton was soundly snubbed and turned away blushing with embarrassment.

The 'Squire' was livid. He waited until after supper, then called for his horse and went charging off into the night. He managed to find out that the orchid had been grown in the conservatory of a great house 25 miles away. When he arrived, he crept in, picked an even more exotic specimen, and rode back again. Handing it to the astonished beauty, he claimed the next waltz. By that time, he had been been in the saddle for four hours and was mud-stained and sweating profusely; but he carried on dancing till dawn.

Money mattered little to Osbaldeston and he seems to have been cheated all through his life. He inherited a large fortune at an early age, then gambled and frittered it away. Sometimes he lost £3,000 a week at billiards alone. Towards the end of his life he was forced to sell his vast Yorkshire estates.

He ended up living quietly in St John's Wood, London, married to his housekeeper. He had been 'sent to Coventry' by the respectable members of the sporting world for supposedly rigging a race. But the paltry sums his prudent wife gave him as an allowance ensured that he could not indulge his former fancies.

On his death in 1866, the 'Squire' was fondly remembered as 'a great sporting gentleman' by men who vied with one another to tell stories of his daring escapades and to boast of the wagers won or lost on his mad capers.

George Osbaldeston

Chapter
Seven

BEES IN THEIR BONNETS

Once a crackpot gets an idea into his head it becomes extremely difficult to dislodge. Eccentrics hang on to their passionate beliefs through thick and thin . . . like the lady who was determined to prise open Shakespeare's grave . . . and the actor who refused to lie down and die . . .

High-class kleptomania

She collected literary lions and other people's silver

Plump, vivacious Lady Cork, wife of the seventh Earl of Cork and Orrery, was an immensely popular woman who even enchanted that grumpy literary giant, Dr Johnson. But she had one little failing that drove her friends to distraction. This was the unfortunate habit of collecting things that did not belong to her.

So well known was her 'tendency' that when she went out to dinner her hosts would put away their silver and leave out pewter spoons and forks which would be scooped up and hidden in her muff. If she visited friends in the country, her maid, on their return home, would have to gather together all the things she knew did not belong to her mistress and send them back to the house where she had been staying – with humble apologies.

Nobody knew quite when it all started. Throughout her long life – she lived to be 94 – she loved good company, and as one of London's most famous hostesses, seemed content with collecting literary lions. As her more unorthodox collections became well known, however, a society wit was prompted to quip that heaven would be rather boring for poor Lady Cork, because there would be nothing to pinch.

Before marrying Lord Cork in 1786 she was plain Mary Monckton. Her early taste for literature made people think she was going to be something of a blue stocking, but she turned out to be a sparkling wit. She often entertained Dr Johnson at her mother's house in Charles Street, Berkeley Square, and he was, by all accounts, very fond of her.

Fanny Burney, who wrote vivid accounts of 18th-century characters, described her as being 'very short, very fat but handsome, splendidly and fantastically dressed, rouged not unbecomingly yet evidently and palpably desirous of gaining notice and admiration ...'

She certainly gained the admiration of Lord Cork and became his second wife when she was 40. With marriage, her passion for entertaining increased and all the famous people of her day came to her dinners and receptions, among them Lord Byron, Sir Walter Scott, Sheridan and the Prince Regent himself. She went on entertaining in style until well past her 90th birthday.

Her drawing rooms, where the famous gathered, were furnished in rather a peculiar manner. There was nothing else in them apart from dozens of large, handsome armchairs lined up against the walls and made fast in some way, so that it was impossible to move them. It was laughingly suggested that as she herself had difficulty distinguishing between 'mine' and 'thine' she perhaps thought her guests had the same problem.

When Lady Cork went shopping, London tradesmen would never allow their goods to be taken to her carriage for approval, as was the custom with people of wealth and position. They always insisted she went inside the shop and, once there, an assistant was appointed to follow her while she was making purchases.

Once she even stole a hedgehog. It belonged to one of the porters at the hotel where she was staying. Being a pet, and quite tame, it was allowed to run about the entrance hall and caused a lot of amusement. Lady Cork could not resist it. As she was leaving she bent down and whipped it into her handbag. But after only a few miles travelling with the disgruntled, prickly little creature she realized she had made a mistake. At the first stop for refreshment – at a village bakery – she managed to exchange it for a sponge cake. She had convinced the baker that hedgehogs were marvellous for keeping down black beetles, and said she knew bakeries were inundated with such pests!

On another occasion, when leaving a party, she made off with another guest's carriage and kept it for half a day before the irate owner turned up for it. Lady Cork did not apologize but complained that the high steps of the vehicle did not suit her short legs.

She was very proud of her remarkable memory and in her 80s could recite half a book at a time. When she suspected it was beginning to fail she kept a young companion by her side who was referred to simply as 'my memory'.

Sir Joshua Reynolds painted Lady Cork when she was young and dashing, but a sketch of her made by a niece, which still exists, sums up her irrepressible, unrepentant nature far better. Under it is written:
'Look at me
 I'm ninety three
 And all my faculties I keep
 Eat, drink and laugh and soundly sleep.'

Bookseller royal

The self-crowned king of Hay-on-Wye

A single gun-shot fired from a rickety boat on the River Wye on April 1, 1977, signalled the start of a new era for the residents of the small Welsh border town of Hay. Though the salvo did little more than startle the ducks, it meant the beginning of Home Rule and Independence from Great Britain – that is, if you happened to be a supporter of bookseller extraordinary Richard Booth, in future to be known as King Richard I of Hay-on-Wye.

The Mayor and Town Council had pinned up a notice saying they completely disowned him, several elderly local residents had threatened him with umbrellas and others had stated publicly that he was off his head. But he had plenty of support from others who, like he, were sick of bureaucratic rule from outside that seemed to be making the ancient town 'poorer and poorer' and in danger of sinking into obscurity.

On Independence Day they sang 'Hay on Wye, Hay on High....' as their national anthem, to the tune of Colonel Bogey, flew the new Free State flag over the ramparts of King Richard's bookshop, half-roasted an ox (somebody got the cooking time wrong) and cheered as a single-engined plane, hired from the local flying club, came into sight, dipping its wing over the hedges in salute.

It was all very moving, but people kept asking Richard Booth 'Why are you King?'. A rumpled, comfortable looking man of 38 with dishevelled hair and owlish spectacles, he didn't look particularly regal – for one thing, his trousers were held up with a safety pin and his socks were odd.

'Well, I'm the biggest property owner in town for a start,' he would explain, 'and it *was* my idea. It came to me all of a sudden in a pub ... some bright spark said if we were going to be independent we would have to have a king, and who better than Booth?'

King Richard owns Hay Castle, a stately pile started in the 11th century, burned down in 1978 and now being lovingly restored. But, more important, he also owns a chain of shops in Hay which comprise the biggest second-hand book business in the world. He has drenched Hay in literature and attracted buyers and sellers to the town from all over the world. At one point he had an estimated 1¼ million books resting on miles of shelves.

King Richard I of Hay-on-Wye

King Richard's ancestors in the town reach back generations. He had a typical upper-crust start in life, first going to Rugby, which he loathed, then to Oxford, which he found boring. He was always in trouble because he wouldn't conform. To please his father, who wanted him to go into the City and restore the family fortunes, he joined a firm of accountants for three weeks. He left like a shot when his great uncle died, leaving the family mansion, Brynmalin, a few miles from the centre of Hay, to his relieved father. Richard now felt free to do what he wanted. More than anything, he liked books, so he promptly opened his first shop in Hay.

His business flourished. But he could see how many small traders and craftsmen in the little town were being driven out of business by big multiple concerns. He declared war on them. With Independence, he said, they would have the Hay National Loaf, baked by local bakers. There would also be Hay National Ice-Cream. He even concocted a plan to get rid of the Central Electricity Generating Board and instead have dozens of people building wind- and water-powered generators to supply Hay's electricity.

King Richard felt just as strongly about all forms of bureaucracy – 'a tiny place like Hay is swamped with dozens of government departments at work, all choking the life out of it' – and even tried to abolish the Welsh Tourist Board. Nowadays, on Bonfire Night in Hay, instead of burning Guy Fawkes they set light to a wooden figure with a bundle of forms in one hand and a cup of tea in the other.

'You wait and see,' he promised the sceptics. 'There are lots of things we can do to make life better for people in Hay. For one thing, there are too many outsiders fishing in the Wye, paying fees to wealthy landowners, not to the town. We'll cut off their lines ..."' he threatened with a huge grin.

Apart from fine speeches, King Richard had some very practical ideas for raising money for the exchequer. He had passports printed and planned to sell them at 25p to anyone crossing the Wye. He even printed some currency on edible rice paper, but didn't get any further than 50p notes.

But the best money spinner was his unique method of creating an instant aristocracy for his kingdom by selling Dukedoms for £25, Earldoms for £15 and Knighthoods for a mere £1 50p. He found American tourists, especially, couldn't resist the temptation and paid up merrily for the privilege of going home with a title.

Running a kingdom, of course, could not be done single handed. He made his gardener, Charlie, Minister of Agriculture, a neighbour who travelled to Hereford every day, Minister for Foreign Affairs, and 'a chap I met in a pub', Chancellor of the Exchequer. His horse, Waterton, named after the great eccentric traveller and zoologist, became Prime Minister. But it was the appointment of glamorous April Ashley, who lived in a flat above one of his shops, as film censor that caused consternation among the teacups. Furthermore he proceeded to create her Duchess of Offa's Dyke!

Since UDI, Hay-on-Wye has thrived, with more and more people flocking there to buy and sell books and sample a whiff of freedom. Since the Great Day in 1977, the anniversary has been celebrated with considerable panache. In 1978 King Richard declared a national holiday (Hay Day) and invited 200 Gujarati Indians from Leicester, declaring that from then on, Gujarati was the second official language. Another year, April Ashley gave a kimono party and His Majesty, charmed by the grace of all those geishas, considered turning Hay into a Japanese town.

The Major and Corporation never stopped protesting. 'He's made this town a laughing stock ... he's upset a lot of elderly people ... he's a crank.' King Richard just laughed. His reign was established. He now had a royal regalia – an orb made from a ballcock and a sceptre from a piece of copper wire.

The world's worst actor

'God's gift to greasepaint' rewrote Shakespeare

The performance of *Romeo and Juliet* was drawing to its close and Shakespeare's immortal lovers were about to be reunited in death. But strange things were happening on stage. Romeo appeared flourishing a crowbar and the audience sat dumbfounded as he struggled to prise open Juliet's tomb.

Actor Robert Coates had been improving the classics again. He had convinced himself that Shakespeare's original ending was too tame and had rewritten it to suit his talents.

Cheated of the usual tender death scene, the audience was soon on its feet, booing and jeering and throwing orange peel. His fellow actors begged Coates to leave the stage, certain that heavier missiles would follow. But he stood his ground, hurling back insults and catcalls until a distraught manager brought down the curtain.

Scenes like this were to be expected whenever Coates stepped onto the stage in Regency London. He was probably the worst actor in the history of the theatre, but nothing could shake his belief that he was God's gift to greasepaint.

Whenever he appeared, there were riots, uproars, threats of lynching – and gales of laughter. Those who appeared on the same stage with him were often struck dumb with embarrassment or fear. At one performance of *Romeo and Juliet* – his favourite play – Juliet became so terrified by the barracking of the crowd that she clung to a pillar, refusing to let go and shrieking with frustration.

Coates was an exotic figure. He came from Antigua, in the West Indies, where his father was a wealthy merchant. His Creole complexion and black hair made him particularly striking. So did his passion for wearing diamonds.

He fell in love with the theatre as a boy. His determination to act, despite his lack of talent, survived constant ridicule.

His first appearance on the English stage was in 1809. However, it was his playing of Romeo in the fashionable spa town of Bath a year later that made his name. He had designed his costume for the part and his first entrance brought the house down. He came on in a flowing cloak spangled with sequins, voluminous red pantaloons, an enormous cravat and a stylish plumed hat.

He went on to tour the British Isles, creating pandemonium everywhere he appeared.

He constantly forgot his lines, invented scenes as he went along and turned to address the audience whenever he thought it was getting out of hand. If he enjoyed playing a scene, he would quite happily repeat it three or four times. He loved dramatic death scenes and had no qualms about breathing his last several times over. Exasperated playgoers would yell: 'Why don't you die?'

Nothing seemed to daunt him. At his curtain call he was often heard to remark: 'Haven't I done it well!' And he would bow towards the box where his great friend and most constant fan, the Baron Ferdinand de Geramb, sat in splendour.

By sheer persistence, he managed to carry on and would even bribe reluctant theatre managers to allow him to appear. They often took the precaution of hiring policemen to keep law and order.

His fame spread and soon he was playing to packed houses. People would travel great distances to see if he really was as bad as everyone reported. He became such an attraction that even the Prince Regent went to see him.

When he played the part of Lothario in Rowe's *The Fair Penitent* at

Robert Coates

London's Haymarket Theatre, at least a thousand people had to be turned away. They even stormed the·stage-door, offering £5 a ticket if they could stand in the wings.

Inside the theatre, Coates, dressed in a fantastic costume of silver and pink silk sparkling with diamonds, and a hat surmounted by tall white feathers, could hardly be heard. When the moment came for him to die, he drew a large handkerchief from his pocket, spread it on the stage and reverently laid his hat on it so that it would not be spoiled by his fall. The audience exploded with laughter.

At another performance in Richmond, Surrey, his acting was so poor that several people laughed themselves ill and had to be helped outside into the fresh air and treated by a doctor.

Then there was the time he lost a diamond buckle. He noticed it just as he was about to make a dramatic exit. Falling to his knees, he crawled round and round the stage on all fours looking for it. The nearly demented prompter hissed: 'Come off! Come off!' Coates ignored him and went on looking until the buckle was found. He then delivered his line: 'Oh, let me hence. I stand on sudden haste.'

Coates did not confine his performances to the stage. In real life he enjoyed dazzling the public with his remarkable clothes. During the daytime he wore fabulous furs, even in the hottest weather. But it was at nights that he came into his own. When he went to balls and grand receptions he glittered from head to foot with diamond buttons and buckles. He gloried in his nickname, 'Diamond Coates'.

To draw even more attention to himself, he had a special carriage built, a shell-shaped chaise which shimmered with all the colours of the rainbow and was emblazoned with his heraldic device – a cock crowing – and his motto: 'While I live, I'll crow.'

London street urchins would chase after him shouting 'cock-a-doodle-doo' and once, in the theatre, someone threw a live cockerel onto the stage which pecked its way around his feet while he delivered a romantic speech. When he had finished the scene he stood in the wings shouting insults at the box from which the cock had been thrown and threatened its occupants with a sword.

At last, it seems, he decided he had given the British public of his best and could no longer put up with its bad manners. After 1815 he appeared less often and gradually his splendour faded.

Coates was to appear in one last finale. The scene was suitably dramatic. In 1848, at 75, he was struck by a Hansom cab and killed instantly.

Literary grave-digger

To her, Shakespeare was just an illiterate deer-poacher

Had the ghost of Will Shakespeare been loitering in the shadows of Holy Trinity Church, Stratford-upon-Avon one dark September night in 1856, he would have been amazed to see a determined American spinster sitting by his tomb.

A lantern threw a circle of flickering light at her feet and in her hand she held a small, sharp shovel. Peering through the gloom, she read again the inscription on his grave, which warned:

Good frend for Jesus' sake forbeare
To digg the dust encloased heare.

Bleste be ye man that spares thes stones
And curst be he that moves my bones.

Yet that was just what Delia Salter Bacon intended. She was determined to prove that Shakespeare did not, *could not* have written the immortal plays and sonnets. The secret of the true author, she believed, lay buried with him.

Delia Bacon, schoolteacher and drawing-room lecturer, had come all the way from New England to pursue this theory, which had haunted her for years.

She had concluded that Shakespeare's works had been written by an élite Elizabethan committee headed by Sir Francis Bacon. Although not a descendant, Delia was convinced that only a man as brilliant and worldly as Bacon could have conceived plays such as *Hamlet* and *King Lear*.

Her friends, including some leading literary figures, winced when Delia called Shakespeare 'that vulgar, illiterate deer-poacher . . .' But nobody could persuade her otherwise.

Delia was born on February 2, 1811, in the log cabin built by her Puritan father in the skeleton town of Tallmadge, Ohio, which he planned to turn into a pure, devout Utopia. Unfortunately, nobody would join him. He had to sell up and head back to New England, where he tried to earn a living selling Bibles, preaching and teaching. The poor man died in August 1817.

His staunch widow, left without money and with six children to feed, did her best. They were farmed out to wealthier relations or friends. Delia went to the Hartford home of a highly successful lawyer and lived in comfort with his family for nine years, receiving the best education then available for a woman.

At 15, she set out to earn a living. Teaching seemed to be the only suitable profession, so, together with her slightly older sister Julia, she rented a room and started a school for young ladies in Connecticut. It was the first of many. None of them paid and the two young schoolmarms were always in debt.

But Delia had discovered Shakespeare. His plays were the central theme of her lectures. Her genteel young ladies sat wide-eyed while she read *Hamlet* and *Romeo and Juliet* with dramatic passion.

Bored with small town life, she took herself off, at the age of 20, to New York, finding accommodation with a clergyman's widow at 769 Broadway. The school she opened there was no more successful than all the others. But Delia had found a better way of earning a living . . .

She resolved to achieve fame with her pen. Inspired by childhood tales of the Anglo-American Puritans, she wrote a book, *Tales of the Puritans*, which was well received. Further success came when the *Philadelphia Saturday Courier* was awarded a prize of $100 for a story entitled *Love's Martyr*, chosen in preference to one by Edgar Allen Poe.

As an author, she was invited to society functions in New England. She was an attractive, graceful woman with softly waving brown hair, grey-blue eyes and a fine white skin set off by the black dresses she always wore. People were intrigued to find she was a brilliant talker with a most 'unfeminine' wit.

After the failure of her next literary endeavour – a play written in highly florid language with an impossible plot, which was rejected by every publisher – she found her true vocation, as a lecturer in history and literature. She could probably have gone on talking about Shakespeare and the Elizabethan era for the rest of her life but for two traumatic experiences.

First, she was struck by the 'divine revelation' that Will Shakespeare was a fraud. Then, at the vulnerable age of 35, she met the Rev. Alexander McWhorter.

Raising her eyes from her studies one day, she met the dark, compelling gaze of the 23-year-old divinity student and fell hopelessly in love. Unfortunately the pious Yale graduate was also a first-class cad. Attracted by her charms, McWhorter pursued her with 'intent', escorted her in public and flattered her outrageously. When Delia sensibly decided to call the whole thing off because of the difference in their ages, he followed her relentlessly.

Their affair became the talk of the town. Her shocked family, fearing she was already a fallen woman, decided to announce that the couple were engaged. At this, the cowardly McWhorter took to his heels.

The scandal was scorching. Brought to trial before a court of ministers, the reluctant lover faced a charge of 'slander, falsehood and conduct dishonourable to the Christian ministry'. Unfortunately Delia, when asked to testify, dissolved into tears and the bounder was vindicated.

She fled to Ohio to recover from the ordeal and continue her studies. With McWhorter out of the way, she was ready again for Shakespeare. But now, suddenly, her attitude changed.

The truth came in a flash. That middle-class Stratford poacher was merely a front. The plays could only have been produced by the finest minds of the day – men like Sir Francis Bacon, Sir Walter Raleigh and the poet Edmund Spenser. They were all idealists with dangerous democratic ideas, who would have paid with their heads if they had spoken openly. But through 'that player' Shakespeare, their thoughts were recorded for posterity.

Back on the New England lecture circuit, she exploded her bombshell. The proper young misses and their mammas were horrified as she poured scorn on the Bard.

It became a taboo subject with her friends. One mention of Shakespeare and she was off. People she stayed with even hid their copies of his works so as not to encourage her.

But she found one invaluable ally in the giant literary figure, Ralph Waldo

Emerson. She told him she needed to go to England to continue her research but that she had no money. Francis Bacon's letters hinted that vital manuscripts and a will had been buried beneath Shakespeare's grave. She was determined to find them.

Emerson invited her to his spacious white-frame house in Concord, gave her letters of introduction to people in England and put her in touch with a wealthy New Yorker, Charles Butler, who promised to back her research for six months.

On May 14, 1853, Delia stepped aboard the steamship *Pacific* in New York bound for England. In her pocket was a letter from Emerson bidding her 'fare well and fare gloriously'. It also contained an introduction to the great English historian, Thomas Carlyle.

On landing in England, she headed directly for Stratford-upon-Avon, strode down the aisle of Holy Trinity Church and confronted the sculpture of the 'impostor'. One glimpse of the smooth, oval face, neatly trimmed beard and bulbous eyes confirmed her previous impression: this was a half-educated tradesman's son who had got on in the world but never had an ounce of poetry in him.

She found lodgings in London and, thanks to Emerson, received an invitation to tea from Carlyle. When she told him the real purpose of her visit, he exploded. 'Do you mean to say,' he asked her, 'that all the Shakespearean scholars are wrong and *you* are going to put them right?'

'I am,' replied Delia firmly. 'And much as I respect you, Mr Carlyle, I must tell you that you do not know what is really in the plays if you believe that booby wrote them!'

He let out a piercing shriek. 'You should have heard him laugh,' she later wrote to her sister. 'I thought he would take the roof of the house off.'

Yet Carlyle was impressed by her quiet dignity and during her years in England did all he could to help her.

It was three-and-a-half years before she got down to the real purpose of her visit: grave-digging. By that time, Charles Butler's money and patience had evaporated. Emerson had given up hope of getting her into print, and she was reduced to living on scraps, unable to afford a fire to heat her room.

It was now, at her lowest ebb, that another literary angel fluttered into her life. Nathaniel Hawthorne, the famous American writer, was serving as United States consul in Liverpool, and she wrote to him, explaining her plight and begging him to read her manuscript.

Aware of the loneliness she must be suffering, he was soon deeply embroiled in her affairs and, though by no means wealthy, sent her money.

One day, being in London, he decided to call on her. He found her lodging with a grocer and his wife, living in rooms above their shop.

On her desk lay a copy of Francis Bacon's letters. She told him they contained definite and minute instructions as to how to find a will and other documents in the hollow space beneath the top stones of Shakespeare's grave. Hence the terrible warning on the tomb.

Hawthorne resolved to get her book published. She never knew the extent of his efforts on her behalf or the money put into it, but by the beginning of April 1857 it was in print and she awaited the world's judgment.

The expected acclaim didn't come. Most reviewers could make neither head nor tail of it. The rest thought it was downright sacrilege.

She had actually dared to address the Bard as 'traitor' and 'miscreant' and demanded to know what he had done with the original manuscripts. 'What *did* you do with them?' she demanded. 'The awakening ages will put you on the stand and you will not leave it until you answer the question. *What did you do with them?*'

Literary historians were appalled by the authorship theory. Where, they demanded to know, was her proof? Even Hawthorne put his foot in it by suggesting her theories were 'romantic'.

Delia, dismayed by this attitude to her life's work, decided it was time for her to go grave-digging.

She had found lodgings with a Mrs Terrett in College Street, Stratford-upon-Avon and soon began to haunt Holy Trinity Church, going there after dark with a candle or lantern, when all the sightseers had gone home and the church was empty.

'You will promise not to disturb anything, madam,' urged the verger, nervously.

'I do faithfully promise,' she assured him, with a tired smile.

The vicar of Holy Trinity, impressed by her sincerity, eventually agreed to let her open the grave. But he made her give her word that she would not touch the coffin itself or harm its contents.

One September night she decided the moment for action had come. She had already confided in her landlady and now she asked Mrs Terrett to act as her accomplice.

They entered the church together after dark but Mrs Terrett was so frightened that she handed Delia the shovel and fled. Delia gathered her skirts around her, set her lantern on the floor and crouched on the stones to read again ... 'And curst be he that moves my bones'. She too was frightened, both by the task she had set herself and by the daunting darkness. Suddenly there was a rustle and a swift patter of feet. The hair on the back of her delicate New England neck rose in horror. But it was only the verger hovering in the shadows. He promised to leave her alone and to return later.

Hours went by. The only sound was the ticking of a clock somewhere and mice scuffling in the dust. Her resolution began to falter. What, she asked herself, if she raised the stone and found *nothing*, absolutely nothing?

What if she had misunderstood Bacon? There was a distinct reference to a tomb in his letters – but did he after all mean his *own* tomb? Were the papers he referred to buried with *his* bones?

Slowly the awful truth dawned.... She couldn't bring herself to do it. When the verger returned she was still sitting there. Without a word, she handed him the shovel and walked slowly down the aisle and into the night. It was the end of everything she had worked for and she was exhausted.

Her mind began to give way. She suffered from delusions. But she loved Stratford, an idyllic place in those days, and took up fresh lodgings in the High Street, writing to Hawthorne, 'I am a great deal more at home here than in America.'

Poor Delia was not allowed to stay long. Her mind was now so disturbed that she was removed to an asylum and eventually taken home to her family.

Only a few people read her book, among them Mark Twain, who was converted and could talk of nothing else for weeks. Her arguments have been used by Baconites ever since.

Delia Bacon died quite calmly and with a clear mind on September 2, 1859. As she slowly faded from this life, not once did she mention Will Shakespeare.

The celestial bed

Dr Graham's easy cure for marital problems

One of the wonders of the medical world in 18th-century London was a Scottish physician named Dr James Graham who invented a 'celestial bed' which, he claimed, would assist childless couples to become more fruitful.

Dr Graham, who left his practice in Edinburgh to open a Temple of Health for a more worldly clientele in London's Adelphi Terrace, believed that invigorating the body with waves of magnetism and electricity would cure most things – including impotence.

Dr. Graham lecturing in Edinburgh

His celestial bed was a magnificent piece of furniture, decorated with cherubs and standing on eight brass legs. Childless couples were charged fees of up to £500 for the chance of spending a night together between its silken sheets. He put his faith in about 15 cwt of compound magnets attached to the bed and, as he put it, 'continually pouring forth in an everlasting circle'.

Dr Graham's fame began to spread in the 1770s. Many said he was a quack but he believed implicitly in what he was doing. He also believed in charging for it. His first Temple at the Adelphi was followed by another in Pall Mall. The emphasis was on soft lights and sweet music. No expense was spared on the lavish furnishings. Dr Graham dealt with sexual problems, fading beauty and nerves in treatment rooms that resembled boudoirs.

Horace Walpole, who visited the first Temple in August 1780, reported that among many astonishing experiences he heard an invisible woman 'warbling to clarinets on the stairs'.

Certainly, Dr Graham believed in posing plenty of scantily draped Greek goddesses all over the place. One of them was the beautiful Emma Hart, later Lady Hamilton and mistress of Lord Nelson. As his favourite 'Goddess of Health' she was even said to have appeared in no draperies at all and once demonstrated how to take a mud bath in front of an entranced audience. Some people sprang to Emma's defence and said that in fact Graham only exhibited her charms from the neck up, displaying an elaborate coiffure lightly powdered and strewn with pearls, feathers and flowers.

Dr Graham himself was a foppishly elegant man who wore suits of white linen and could be seen walking through the fashionable quarters of London carrying a gold-headed cane in one hand and a posy of flowers in the other.

At his Temple he was attended by negro servants as he administered special baths to his patients, sat them on magnetic thrones and soothed their nerves with music and massage. He did a roaring trade in patent medicines, ointments and pills, which could be bought in three sizes costing 5s, 10s 6d and one guinea.

For a time Dr Graham was all the rage. But he was not admired by everyone. His ideas were scorned by the medical hierarchy of the day, though some of his innovations – mud baths, hypnotism and electric shock treatment, for instance – are in constant use today at expensive hydros and health spas.

He was a religious man and had great belief in prayer. When George III became seriously ill, he wrote out a prayer on a piece of paper and asked that it should be pinned to the King's pillow.

Despite the enormous sale of his potions and the fascination of his treatments, the novelty of what he offered began to fade. He was eventually forced to accept that London had not been converted to his theories and back he went to sober Edinburgh. He kept on preaching about the virtues of magnetism and electricity until the Scots, equally fed up with him, locked him up as a lunatic.

Chapter
Eight

SARTORIAL SCREWBALLS

Vanity over clothes has never been the monopoly of women. Men have been among the dottiest of dressers. There was the Irish farmer who always wore white linen and even refused to have black cattle in his fields; and Beau Brummell, the dandy who would take three hours to tie his cravat and immortalized the phrase, 'Who's your fat friend?'

Gold dresses and buns

Brilliant poetess who shocked her audiences

Looking down her long, thin nose, Edith Sitwell would inform her admirers: 'I am, of course, descended from the Plantagenets . . .' The connection was actually rather distant and she looked uncannily like the Tudor Queen Elizabeth I. But anyone who saw her could not help but be devastatingly impressed.

Six feet tall with a pale, lofty forehead and hooded eyes, she had one of the most famous faces of her age. As the acknowledged High Priestess of English poetry, her public appearances were sensational. She loved to dress in great sweeping gowns of stiff brocade or velvet decorated with semi-precious stones. She wore gold turbans and painted her finger nails to match. Vast topaz and acquamarine rings glittered on her hands, bracelets of amber and jet clattered round her wrists and her chest was usually weighted down with an enormous cross or an Aztec collar in beaten gold.

Behind the public facade, however, was an ugly duckling, who had vowed that being 'plain' would never stop her from making an impact on the world.

Edith was born on September 7, 1887, at gloomy, haunted Renishaw Hall in Derbyshire, ancestral home of the Sitwell family. Her mother, Lady Ida, was a ravishing 18-year-old beauty who had been forced to marry the eccentric Sir George Sitwell. She was utterly dismayed when she saw the child she had produced and did her best to ignore her.

'My childhood was hell,' Edith told everyone years later. It was certainly very lonely until her two brothers, Osbert and Sacheverell, were born. She coped by retreating into a private world of poetry and books.

There were continual battles and emotional storms between the baronet and his flighty wife and one enormous family upheaval when Lady Ida got herself into the hands of money lenders and subsequently, Holloway prison. Sir George or 'Ginger', as his children referred to him, was only really interested in two things – the Sitwell name and money. When he noticed that Edith apparently had a slight curvature of the spine, he had her shackled into an iron frame every night to try to cure it. It didn't do a bit of good and made her even more furious.

Somehow she remained undaunted by the Sitwell upbringing. When a family friend asked her what she wanted to be when she grew up, five-year-old Edith replied: 'A genius.' Teenage Edith rebelled with spirit. When her parents took her to the smart races, she sat with her back to the course; she managed to be violently sick at a brass band concert in the Albert Hall and she took to wearing long black velvet dresses when all the nice girls were in white tulle. 'If one is a greyhound, why try to look like a Pekingese?' she asked tartly.

Edith endured life at Renishaw until she was 25; then, to her intense relief, she was allowed to pack her bags and go off to London with her governess, Helen Rootham, as chaperone. Renishaw may have been gloomy, but life had been luxurious. Now she happily lived in a scruffy fourth-floor flat in Pembridge Mansions, Bayswater, on a diet of soup, beans and buns. She was free.

Dame Edith Sitwell on her way to Hollywood

From this moment on her whole life was devoted to becoming a major poet. Her first poem 'Drowned Suns' was published in the *Daily Mirror* that spring. She was paid the grand sum of £2 but retained an affection for the *Mirror* for the rest of her life.

Within a decade she had achieved respect, notoriety and fame. With her brothers, literary lions Osbert and Sacheverell, she made up a trio that amazed and intrigued everyone. Witty and clever, theatrically draped in flowing black capes, they were unique.

Edith's flat became the meeting place for half literary London. Aldous Huxley, Virginia Woolf, T.S. Eliot, Dylan Thomas ... they all staggered up those four flights of dreary concrete stairs to be greeted by the High Priestess. They found nothing waiting for them but strong tea in mugs and Edith's interminable buns. She excused herself from inviting anyone to dinner by saying 'The cooking is too primitive ...'

Soon she was heading into a storm of public derision. In 1923, with composer William Walton, she wrote a surrealist entertainment in verse called 'Facade'. The whole thing was performed behind a curtain with a hole through which her words were recited with the aid of a large megaphone. It was a disaster. Nobody understood it and the entire experience, with Edith's voice swooping up and down behind the curtain, was too much for some of the audience. Noel Coward, for instance, went away and wrote a sketch entitled 'The Swiss Family Whittlebot' in which Hernia Whittlebot recited abstruse poems with her two brothers, Gob and Sago. Edith retired to bed with jaundice and wouldn't speak to Coward for 40 years. Later, of course, 'Facade' became a brilliant success.

By the age of 40 Edith was thoroughly enjoying her role as a celebrity. Cecil Beaton had finally laid the ghost of her parents' tactless remarks about her 'plain' looks by declaring that he thought her quite beautiful and photographing her over and over again – once in a coffin! Her public appearances became more and more extraordinary. For one recital she wore a Chinese coat of gold flecked wth green over a black satin dress, and topped it off with a Tudor hat, studded with gold and framed by two drifting lengths of black chiffon. Everything about her glinted and clanked. Nobody could have guessed that her favourite night out was a visit to the music hall to hear Nellie Wallace, followed by a steak and onion supper, washed down with beer!

Her life was punctuated with glorious rows and threats to sue all and sundry. Though kind and generous at heart, she was also very prickly. For instance, she loathed D. H. Lawrence because she was convinced that he had used Renishaw Hall as the setting for *Lady Chatterley's Lover*. In retaliation she said his poetry was 'soft, woolly and hot ... like a Jaeger sweater', whereupon

Dame Edith Sitwell rehearsing for her 75th birthday concert

Jaeger threatened to sue *her* for saying their sweaters were hot!

She never married but fell passionately in love with impossible men. Her most intense romance was with the bi-sexual Russian painter, Tchelitchew, who accused her of behaving like Joan of Arc and almost broke her heart. Equally stormy were her relationships with some of her young protégés, among them Dylan Thomas, who was frightened of meeting her at first but eventually became almost like a son. His exasperating behaviour, especially when drunk, caused her to threaten: 'He is rapidly heading for having his ears boxed. . . .' At one point she cut him out of her life for eight years, but forgave him everything 'because he is the greatest poet of his generation'.

During the Second World War Edith and Osbert retired to Renishaw to write by the light of oil lamps. As her war effort she would spend hours knitting strange garments for any of their friends serving in the forces. Alec Guinness, the actor, received a pair of seaboot stockings soon after he joined the navy, described as 'very long and curiously shaped with two left feet'.

The later years of her life had the same bravura as her youth. In 1948, when she was 61, she sailed for America with Osbert and Sacheverell and travelled the States reading her poetry and performing 'Facade' in a great gold dress that swept the floor. The American audiences were hypnotized. In turn, she adored America and especially Hollywood, where she got on well with Marilyn Monroe and went sightseeing in an ankle-length fur coat and black sandals.

Back home in 1954, she was made a Dame of the British Empire and was touched to realize that she had become an 'institution' treasured by the public. She could still be totally outrageous. Having written a highly acclaimed book on Queen Victoria, she referred to the monarch as 'that old bore'.

Confined to a wheelchair in her 70s, she continued to hold court in a comfortable flat in Hampstead, cared for by her private secretary and companion, Elizabeth Salter. On her visits to London she was driven round in a Daimler and, however overdrawn at the bank, gave two parties a day at her favourite restaurant.

Her last public poetry reading was in 1962, only two years before her death. She insisted on referring to the event as her 'memorial concert'. Preparations were as elaborate as ever and her wardrobe chosen with the greatest care. She appeared on stage in her wheelchair, wearing a red velvet dress with red satin sleeves and the great gold Aztec collar used for ceremonial occasions. Her hat was gold, her shoes gold and her ring-laden fingers tipped with scarlet. The 'Plantagenet' Edith must have been well satisfied. She was treated like royalty.

Transvestite diplomat

The Queen's representative who wore petticoats

When Queen Anne sent her cousin, Lord Cornbury, to represent her in America as Governor of New York and New Jersey, he took her quite literally.

Guests at the opening of the New York Assembly in 1702 were astounded when the English aristocrat made his entrance in a fashionable blue silk gown, an elegant headdress studded with diamonds, and satin shoes. Even worse – he was carrying a fan!

Furious diplomats complained that Lord Cornbury had made them a laughing stock. His reply, in his own opinion, was perfectly logical: 'You are all very stupid people not to see the propriety of it all. In this place and on this occasion, I represent a woman, and in *all* respects I ought to represent her as faithfully as I can.'

Not that Lord Cornbury, third Earl of Clarendon, needed much excuse to indulge in his favourite hobby – dressing in high feminine fashion – though nobody at that time seemed to think his taste perverted, just odd.

He had started collecting women's clothes when he was eight years old and was often seen about town in them. He always employed the most fashionable dressmakers, milliners and shoemakers. His vast wardrobe of beautiful gowns, wigs, fans and stockings rivalled that of any courtesan. He had outfits for morning, afternoon and evening of an astonishing variety, a good many of which were sent to him by the Queen herself.

Lord Cornbury was hardly suited to play a feminine role. He was a large man with a fleshy, masculine face quite out of keeping with lace boudoir bonnets and silk petticoats. Nevertheless, he carried out his eccentricity to the full, even lacing himself into 'stays' to give himself a figure.

Far from keeping his hobby a secret, he loved to show off his clothes and boast of what they cost him. By contrast, he was so mean to his wife that she was driven to steal. He would often go out onto the streets of New York at night wearing a hooped skirt and powdered wig, or he would sit at an open window fanning himself to the great amusement of his neighbours. On one occasion he actually left a reception being given in his honour in order to change his dress.

Cornbury served as Governor in New York from 1701 to 1708 but was said

Lord Cornbury

to be hopelessly inefficient as an administrator and an incurable spendthrift. Hard-headed American businessmen had also made it clear they did not appreciate having to conduct their affairs with a burly man dressed in frills and furbelows.

He was recalled to England in 1708, arrested, and kept in custody until he paid his debts. But he was undoubtedly a clever man and quickly rose to power again, being made a member of Queen Anne's Privy Council in 1711. However, old ways die hard and a Mr Williams was reported as having seen a picture of him at Sir Herbert Packington's in Worcestershire 'in a gown, stays, tucker, long ruffles and cap....'

King of the dandies

Beau Brummell took three hours to tie his cravat

Beau Brummell took his seat at the candlelit table without looking to left or right. He was dining in distinguished company. His servant whispered the information that on one side of him was the Marquis of Headfort and on the other was Lord Yarmouth.

For the rest of the evening Brummell entertained the two aristocrats with a conversation of devastating wit – without once turning his head.

Brummell had no intention of disturbing one fold of his exquisitely arranged cravat. It had, after all, taken him three hours to tie!

George 'Beau' Brummell, king of the dandies in Regency England, made the cravat his trademark. A snowy froth of fine, starched muslin, it created a sensation when he first wore it.

One speck of dust, one crease, and a cravat was tossed aside and the whole ritual of tying it would begin again. The floor of his dressing room was often littered ankle-deep with yards of discarded muslin. 'These are our failures,' explained his valet.

Brummell lived for the art of dressing. His style influenced an age and made him a legend. He would not leave his room until the figure he saw reflected in the mirror was groomed to ultimate perfection.

Three people were involved in making his gloves, one specializing in the

George 'Beau' Brummell

thumb alone. His valet polished the soles of his boots as well as the uppers. Once, when a friend asked him what blacking he used to give his boots such a magnificent shine, Brummell exclaimed: 'Blacking! I never use blacking. I use nothing but the froth of champagne.'

He became such a symbol of elegance that the Prince of Wales would call at Brummell's home in Chesterfield Street just to watch him dress. The incredible 'Beau' wielded great influence over the Prince, whom he called 'Prinny', and the fashions of his court. Once when Brummell told him bluntly that he did not like the cut of his coat, 'Prinny' burst into tears.

Brummell, ironically, was the grandson of a valet. The rise in the family's status was due entirely to the efforts of Brummell's father, William. His first job was as a government clerk, but he married a wealthy heiress. William Brummell eventually became private secretary to Lord North, prime minister of England.

He made enough money to send the budding Beau, his youngest son, to Eton and Oxford where he acquired a taste for aristocratic friends. However, it was on a visit to London that the turning point came in Brummell's life. He met the Prince of Wales who was captivated by the young dandy's charm and elegance. The Prince promised Brummell a commission in his own regiment when he had finished his studies.

Brummell was astute enough to realize that a commission in the exclusive 10th Light Dragoons would admit him to the cream of society. He accepted, and soon was mixing with the sons of dukes and earls.

Though he looked dazzling in Hussar uniform, he was not a good officer. He hated being away from London and Brighton, where he could display himself to the best advantage.

The last straw seemed to be when his regiment was ordered to Manchester. 'I really could not go,' he told the Prince. 'Think, your Royal Highness, Manchester! Besides, you would not be there.'

By now the Prince was completely won over. 'Oh by all means Brummell,' he answered. 'Do as you please.'

Brummell bought himself out of the Army. From then on, all his attention and energy was devoted to his exquisite self and to that rich, self-indulgent society in which the dandy was king.

Brummell was not particularly handsome. He had reddish fair hair, thick lips which he liked to pout, and cool eyes. But his figure was perfectly proportioned and his elegance unsurpassed.

When he made his debut in London, men were ludicrously overdressed. They did not think it necessary to wash before putting on their lace-edged finery. Brummell brought in a revolution. His clothes were simple, plain and subdued – but they were perfect. His whole secret was simplicity and cleanliness.

It took him two hours to wash. After shaving he would pluck out any offending hair with a pair of silver tweezers. Before dressing he scrubbed his whole body with a stiff brush until he was 'red as a lobster'.

He never wore perfume. Instead he changed his shirt three times a day and sent his linen to be laundered in the country so that it should 'smell of new-mown hay'. His laundry bills were astronomical.

When he had dressed for the evening he would refuse to set foot on the pavement. Instead, his sedan chair, with its white satin lining and soft white sheepskin rugs, would be brought to the foot of the stairs in his house. He could then arrive at his destination as perfect as when he had torn himself away from the mirror.

One weekend he went to stay at a magnificent country house. His friend asked whether he had enjoyed himself. 'Don't ask me, my dear fellow,' groaned Brummell. 'I actually found a cobweb in my night pot!' After that traumatic event he took to keeping a folding chamberpot in a mahogany case for travelling.

Women adored him but he is believed to have remained celibate. He would not raise his hat to a woman in the street in case he was not able to replace it at exactly the right angle.

One liaison he considered ended abruptly. 'What could I do?' he sighed. 'I discovered that Lady Mary actually ate cabbage.' He loathed vegetables, though he had a farm labourer's appetite for bread and cheese.

Brummell ruled London with his fantastic sense of style for 18 years. He had all that time been a close favourite of the Prince, who had become Regent.

But the exquisite dandy had watched his royal patron grow fat and ungainly, and thinking himself in an impregnable position, he used his sharp wit to poke fun at him. Friends warned him to be careful but he took no notice.

One day, strolling along Bond Street with Lord Alvanley, he came face to face with the Prince, who chatted amiably to Alvanley and ignored Brummell. As the stout figure laced into its royal corsets turned to go, Brummell fired his famous salvo: 'Alvanley, who's your fat friend?'

The Prince never spoke to him again.

Brummell continued to lead the life of a dandy, but finally succumbed to the Regency mania for gambling. In 1816, deep in debt and in danger of arrest, he fled to France, never to return.

For some years, supported by loyal friends, he managed to carry on in some style, running up gigantic bills with his tailor and laundress. But in the end he had only the ghosts of his brilliant past and mirages of splendours long gone.

Brummell's last home was the spartan and infinitely unfashionable Caen Lunatic Asylum. He died there in 1840, aged 62.

White for all occasions

Linen Cook, the humane health-addict

The 17th-century Irish farmer Robert Cook was the most startling figure in County Waterford. He never wore anything but white linen.

Not only were his underclothes, night clothes and shirts in purest white, but so were his suits, coats and hats. He became so famous for his clothes and his passion for white that he was known all over Ireland as 'Linen Cook'.

He refused to have any black cattle in the fields of his farm at Cappoquin and even his horses had to be the same pure white as his clothes.

Cook was a passionate vegetarian and refused to eat the flesh of any animal or to wear anything produced by an animal.

A fox which attacked his poultry was not killed when it was caught. Instead, he gave it a lecture on the evils of murder, then offered it a sporting chance by making it run through a line of his farm labourers, who were armed with sticks.

Cook had a long and healthy life, finding that 'water for drink and pulse, corn and other vegetatives for food and linen and other vegetatives for raiment be sufficient'.

He died in 1726 when he was over 80 years old and was buried in a white linen shroud.

Clown of Rock

His pranks cost him a fortune

Hotel managers the world over said a silent prayer when they heard that Keith Moon was coming to stay. Moon, wild-eyed drummer with 'The Who' Rock group had earned a reputation as the supreme joker of the pop world. Hotels were his favourite target and he didn't care a damn how much his escapades cost.

He had been known to drop a firecracker down the loo in an American hotel, blowing a great hole in the bathroom floor. Once, when a frantic manager complained about the loud music coming from his room, he blasted the door off. He took an axe to furniture, hurled TV sets through windows and, for a period of 10 years, happily wrecked hotel bedrooms in America, Europe and the Far East. His extraordinary behaviour cost him between £150,000 and £200,000 in damages!

To many people's surprise, Keith Moon could explain himself articulately: 'The momentum is still there when I come off stage. I'm like an express train or an ocean liner. It takes me two or three miles to stop.' Regarded as a clown, albeit a destructive one, he was in many ways the victim of his own reputation. He came to feel everyone *expected* him to be outrageous. Once asked what he feared most he admitted, 'Having to grow up'.

Being his friend let you in for some hair-raising experiences. He made Mick Jagger furious on his honeymoon. The 'Rolling Stones' lead singer and his wife Bianca had gone to bed and were asleep in their 11th-floor hotel room in Hollywood. Jagger was wakened by a rustling movement on the balcony outside and the sound of heavy breathing. He drew a gun from under his pillow and aimed it, thinking they were about to be burgled. Just in time, he heard a familiar voice drawl 'good evening'. It was Keith Moon, come to offer his congratulations. He had climbed to the 11th storey from balcony to balcony and collapsed with laughter while Jagger, understandably, fumed.

Actor Steve McQueen found it was something of an ordeal living next door to him in Malibu. Moon kept a telescope trained on McQueen's beautiful wife, Ali McGraw, and would sometimes go roaring across the film star's lawn on a motor bike. It was all part of his plan to discomfort the superior 'jet set' of Hollywood.

At home in America or at his smart mews house in London's Mayfair, he could be seen relaxing in a black-velvet, monogrammed dressing gown, swigging Bucks Fizz (champagne and orange juice) out of a mug, like a Regency hell-raiser, born out of time.

Keith Moon, son of a London motor mechanic, was born on August 23, 1947, and all his early years were spent around Wembley and Shepherd's Bush. He went from one job to another until he joined 'The Who', then known under a different name, in the 1960s. He said quite plainly he thought their drummer was no good and that he could do better. When he turned up for his audition, lead singer Roger Daltrey remembers he had orange hair and wore a bright orange suit; so they called him 'the gingerbread man'. His audition ended with a crashing finale in which he managed to smash his drum kit to pieces. The group thought he was great. He was hired.

They soon found he was the sort of man who created mayhem out of nothing. Outrageous stories were always circulating about him, some of them quite untrue. But Moon in top gear was a force to be reckoned with. There was a time when he would polish off two bottles of brandy and two of champagne every day, 'just to get things moving'. He once dumped a new Lincoln Continental car in a hotel swimming pool, then sat back and waited for the reaction.

Sometimes his fellow musicians would take to their hotel rooms for a bit of peace and quiet. On one occasion when that happened and they refused to let him in, he used an explosive device to blow the doorknobs off.

He spent his money as fast as he earned it. Being court jester to the pop world was an expensive business. His great weakness was for dressing up. He would go out into the street in anything from a nun's habit to a Nazi storm-trooper's uniform. One afternoon in London's Oxford Street, a lilac Rolls Royce drew up to the kerb and two scar-faced hoodlums in trilbies and striped suits leaped onto the pavement. They headed straight for a bald, middle-aged clergyman, who seemed to be minding his own business, and treated him to a roughing up that would have done justice to an early James Cagney film. Passers-by looked on appalled – as passers-by usually do. The poor vicar was dragged, struggling and kicking into the Rolls and was heard to yell: 'Have you no respect for the Cloth?' While most people stood rooted to the spot with horror as the car drew away, two young men gave chase and saw the abducted vicar pinned down in the back seat, arms and legs thrashing. The car was stopped at a police road block and the unfortunate clergyman released. It was Keith Moon.

Grinning his gap-toothed grin and ruffling his already dishevelled hair, he would plead: 'I love the unexpected – and I love to make people laugh.'

His favourite prank was what he called 'The Trouser Joke'. He would go

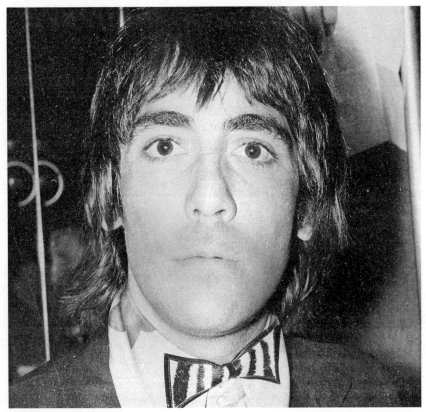

Keith Moon of 'The Who'

into a store and ask for a specially strong pair of trousers. A customer who happened to be passing – by arrangement of course – would be asked to help test the trousers before he bought them. They would take a leg apiece and rip the trousers apart. Moon's road manager would then appear on crutches, with one leg cunningly strapped out of sight. 'Ah, that's just what I want,' he would cry out on spotting the single trouser leg. Moon would insist that he accepted both legs as a gift, but insisted that they were wrapped separately. He would then solemnly pay the bill and depart.

He had a passion for explosives. In America, when 'The Who' appeared on TV, it was decided their performance must end with something memorably dramatic. What could be more dramatic than Keith Moon's drums exploding on the final note of their last number? When the time came, the special effects man arrived with his gunpowder and set up the operation. Unfortunately, according to Keith Moon himself, 'I kept giving the special effects man more and more drink from my hip flask and he kept putting more and more gunpowder into my drum kit.' When it came to the last note, Moon gave the cue and all hell broke loose. He was hurled backwards through the scenery by the violence of the explosion and lead guitarist Peter Townshend was left standing petrified, his hair on fire. Moon staggered forward to make his bow, covered in blood, with bits of cymbals sticking out of his arms. Screen star, Bette Davis, waiting in the wings with Mickey Rooney, took one look at Moon and fainted.

Considering his unprepossessing looks – he was usually half-shaved and bleary eyed – he fascinated women of all kinds from wide-eyed hangers-on to smart society girls. He married his wife, Kim, when he was only 18 and she 16. For publicity reasons, he was persuaded to keep his marriage secret and to pretend that Kim was his sister. Not surprisingly, the marriage ended in divorce.

One night Moon was having a meal at 'Tramp', a fashionable West End haunt for show people, when he saw a beautiful blonde Swedish girl at a nearby table. He was completely bowled over. Calling a waiter, he gave him a substantial tip and arranged for the blonde's escort to be called away. Then he went over and introduced himself to Annette Walter-Lax. If she was angry, she didn't show it. Such was Keith Moon's effect that their relationship carried on from there. She went to live in California with him and nearly succeeded in taming him. Marriage? 'I'm married to "The Who",' he once said emphatically. 'After all the pressures we've been through we're welded together ...' But friends say he would have married Annette Walter-Lax had he lived.

Moon always predicted that he would die young, so perhaps that was why he was so reckless. With the help of the Swedish girl and the moral support of fellow drummer, Beatle Ringo Starr, he managed to curb his drinking. But he still regarded himself as the Clown Prince and only two months before he died he was thrown off a British Airways jet in the Seychelles when he tried to break into the pilot's cabin and play his drumsticks on the control panel.

One night in 1978 he went to a party. He was in a quiet mood, spent most of his time talking music with Beatle Paul McCartney, and announced his engagement to Annette. Next morning, he was found dead; and although there was talk of a drug overdose all those closest to him insisted he had died in his sleep of natural causes. One thing would have pleased him. He was last seen in public with a glass of champagne in his hand and a beautiful girl on his arm. It had been a great performance.

The mad Marquis

He doled out free gin in the Haymarket

One of the greatest practical jokers of all time was the flamboyant third Marquis of Waterford, known in his day as 'Wild Lord Waterford' or 'The Mad Marquis'.

He inherited a fortune in the early 19th century but managed to squander a great deal of it on financing and paying the damages for his eccentric pranks.

On one occasion he took it upon himself to distribute strong liquor to the deserving London poor. Descending on a famous tavern in the Haymarket, he ordered the innkeeper to roll several casks of gin onto the pavement and then stood there distributing half-pint mugs to passers-by.

Soon he was surrounded by half the rogues and vagabonds in London who had scented a free drink streets away. Drunken riots followed and the police only managed to extricate his lordship by arresting him.

His brushes with the law were often comic. Once he was summoned to appear at Marlborough Street court on a charge of driving his horse and carriage through a crowded thoroughfare at a reckless and dangerous speed. He arrived for the hearing on horseback, rode up the court house steps and demanded to be let in. The horse, he said, was a witness for the defence. He demanded that it should be cross-examined 'because only he knows how fast he was going'. Faced with such lunatic logic, the judge decided to rid himself of the case as fast as possible and acquitted him.

Waterford was very fond of showing off on his horse. On several occasions he charged up the steps of the Kilkenny Hunt Clubhouse and laughed uproariously when officials tried to throw him out. He couldn't stand the fashionable people who daily trotted up and down London's famous Rotten Row and once dressed up as a workman and drove a water cart in and out of the mounted dandies.

Nor did he have time for pomp. Having rented him a house, the owners were furious when they returned and found he had shot out the eyes of all the family portraits. At his own estate at Curraghmore, County Waterford, he stuck a cigar in the mouth of one of his most illustrious ancestors.

Some of his jokes were destructive, but he always made good the damage.

For instance, he once sat on 22 hats in a fashionable milliner's shop – all of them specially created for a big occasion. Waterford was convulsed with laughing when the milliner returned and amid much weeping and wailing declared she was a ruined woman. The Marquis explained he just couldn't resist the temptation and handed her a handsome cheque.

His friends had to be prepared for anything. A guest of the Marquis once found himself getting into bed with a donkey. When life became dull he thought up a new prank. Once he hired eight cabs and persuaded a whole tribe of musicians to sit on the roofs playing like fury while they were driven in procession round the streets. Waterford took the reins of the leading cab, inviting all and sundry to climb aboard and have a ride. The pace got faster and the noise louder until everyone thought he would be killed in the pandemonium.

But he survived all his wild pranks, only to break his neck in a mundane hunting accident in 1859.

The midas touch

A fortune from warming pans and whalebone

Self-made American millionaire Timothy Dexter made his fortune by selling coals to Newcastle and warming pans to the West Indies. The crazier his business ideas, the better they worked.

Snobbish New Englanders laughed at Dexter for his nouveau riche ways, his eccentric manners and odd appearance. But he usually managed to have the last laugh where money was concerned.

He was born into a very poor family in Malden, Massachusetts, on January 2, 1747, and had very little schooling (he never learned to spell). At eight he was working as a farm labourer. At 16 he decided to better himself and became an apprentice in the smelly trade of leather-dressing. From then on, nothing could stop him.

He arrived in 1769 at Newburyport, a thriving harbour 40 miles from Boston with only a few dollars in his pocket and his worldly goods in a bundle. He soon set himself up in the trade he had been taught and within a year had acquired a wife, a splendid house and a thriving business. His bride, a rich widow called Elizabeth Frothingham, obviously knew a winner when she saw one.

It was at the end of the War of Independence in 1783 that his genius for trade became apparent. He bought up a large amount of European currency which, due to the cessation of trade during the war, was almost valueless in America. As stability returned he found himself in possession of a fortune. He had two ships built and began to export goods to Europe and the West Indies. His wealth increased and his fame grew as his transactions became more and more bizarre.

Some mischievous merchant clerks goaded him into making a huge investment in warming pans for the West Indies. But it so happened that the captain of his ship was an ingenious fellow and sold the pans as ladles for the huge West Indian molasses industry. Dexter made a handsome profit on the deal.

Another time he sent a shipload of warm, woolly mittens to the same sweltering islands. He struck lucky again. They were snapped up by merchants from Asia and exported to the frozen wastes of Siberia!

Everyone thought Timothy Dexter was good for a laugh, but New England businessmen nearly choked over their claret when they heard he had sent his ships off to England, loaded with coal for Newcastle. Some practical joker had told him there was a desperate need for it on Tyneside and, not being an educated man, he didn't know that Newcastle was then one of the biggest coal centres in the world.

By one of those strokes of luck that could only happen to Dexter, Newcastle was in the throes of a coal strike when his ships arrived and instead of being sent packing he was greeted with open arms. Enormous bids were made for his cargo and his profits were vast. In his diary he wrote, 'I was very lucky in spekkelation ...'

Next, he bombarded the East Indies with Bibles, together with a text explaining that anyone not owning a Bible was sure to go to hell. He was said to have profited by 47,000 dollars on that little deal. He also exported stray cats to the Caribbean islands where vermin were out of control. Large warehouse owners purchased them for as much as five dollars a head.

At one time he stocked up to bursting point with whalebone, after hearing a refitter who was working on one of his ships complain one day that it was almost impossible to buy enough 'stay stuff'. The refitter meant ships' rigging but Dexter misunderstood and thought he was talking about corset stays, some of which were manufactured from whalebone. Dexter immediately set out to corner the whalebone market, buying 342 tons of the stuff.

Everyone declared he had finally gone mad! But the following spring, when the latest Paris fashions arrived by boat, they included huge skirts and long corsets that demanded yards and yards of whalebone. And who had the monopoly on whalebone? That poor fool Dexter, of course.

He considered – quite rightly – that he had done rather well for himself. But the New England snobs closed their ranks and ignored him. He retaliated by buying up one of the very best houses in Newburyport, a large brick mansion in State Street with a sweeping staircase and gilded mirrors. The top families were struck speechless. Its previous owner had been one Nathaniel Tracy, a gentleman of the kind that Boston understood, who entertained with elegance, employed liveried negro slaves and kept a magnificent wine cellar. Dexter tried to copy him – with hilarious results. Sadly, no one came to visit him and no one asked him out for dinner.

He was certainly an odd figure in his broad-brimmed cocked hat dancing with tassels, ankle-length coat and breeches tied with ribbons round his shins. His grey hair hung almost to his shoulders, but his face was dominated by a pair of lively, mischievous eyes. He was usually followed by a small, smooth black dog, scarcely bigger than a cat.

Though he could make money like a wizard, his private life was a disaster. His son was a failure, his daughter weak-witted and his wife a nag. He decided the best thing was to pretend she didn't exist and always referred to her in writing as 'the gost'. He introduced her to strangers as 'Mrs Dexter, the gost that was my wife. . . .'

Fed up with the snobs of Newburyport, he felt the only way he could get his own back was by making himself grander and grander. He bought a huge country estate in Chester, New Hampshire and while there acquired a title – nobody knew quite how. He let it be known that in future he was to be referred to as *Lord* Timothy Dexter.

Within a year he was back again, complete with peerage. He told anyone who would listen that his old house in State Street was too cramped and promptly purchased a magnificent Georgian mansion standing on high ground and looking out to sea. He thought it rather plain and decorated the roof with Eastern minarets and gold balls. On top of the cupola he perched a great golden eagle to act as a weather vane. But his master stroke was still to come. He filled his garden with life-size wooden statues of famous men, declaring they were 'better company' than his stuffy neighbours.

He started his 'mouseum' of statues in 1801 and promised, 'I will show the world one of the Grete wonders of the world in 15 months ... that is,' he added, 'if no man murders me in Dors or out of Dors.'

His 'mouseum' consisted of 40 great figures and set pieces made of painted wood (he would have preferred marble). They included sentimental groups with titles like 'Motherly Love' and 'Four Lions Lying Down with a Lamb'; there were Thomas Jefferson, George Washington, Pitt, Bonaparte, Venus and, towering over them all, a statue of himself bearing the inscription, 'I am the first in the East, the first in the West and the greatest philosopher in the Western World.'

At last he gained the attention he craved. People came from all over the country to see his 'mouseum'. They were also taken to see the splendid tomb that Dexter had already built for himself containing a magnificently decorated coffin lined with white lead. Inside the tomb to sustain him on his last journey he had placed a pipe and some tobacco, a supply of fireworks, a speaking trumpet and 'a Bibel to read and sum good songs'.

But Timothy Dexter had still not finished with the snobs who had scorned him. When he was nearly 50 he decided to write a book. It became one of the great curiosities of American literature. The spelling is awful. There are no full stops and capital letters are strewn all over the place. But *A Pickle for the Knowing Ones* or *Plain Truths in a Homespun Dress* was much in demand. Given away at first, it eventually changed hands at quite high prices and ran into eight editions.

His aim was stated clearly: 'I wans to make my Enemys grin in time Like a Cat over A hot pudding and gone Away and hang there heads Down Like A Dogg. . . .'

The book started out to tell the story of his life and to explain what a marvellous fellow he really was, but before long readers were bogged down in a welter of strange facts. He rambled all over the place, launching into attacks on politicians, the clergy and anyone else he didn't particularly like. He discussed 'Bonne partey the grat' (Napoleon), his wife's habit of nagging and 'Dexter's Mouseum', which was to include statues of 'mister pitt', 'the king of grat britton' and 'Loues the 16 of France'.

When people complained that they could hardly understand his deathless prose, he decided to add an extra page to his masterpiece and it was bound into all the later editions. It had nothing on it but punctuation marks. 'The Nowing ones complane of my book the fust edition had no stops I put in A nuf here and they may pepper and salt it as they please,' wrote Dexter, somewhat huffily.

Dexter continued to live with 'the gost' but the great comfort of his life was his enormous negro housekeeper, Lucy, daughter of an African prince. She was aggressively protective and looked after him like a mother hen. He seemed to collect strange characters. His household included a fortune teller, an idiot 6 ft 7 ins tall and a poet laureate, appointed by himself, called Jonathan Plummer, who once earned his living as a fishmonger and dealer in pornographic literature. He seemed to amuse the millionaire, who dressed him ornately in a cocked hat, a black and silver coat and silver-buckled shoes.

Every afternoon Dexter consumed vast quantities of rum and brandy – he didn't touch a drop in the morning when most of his business transactions were carried out. One day, feeling bored, he began to wonder what others would say about him when he died. He decided there was only one way he could find out . . . he announced his death and made elaborate plans for his funeral.

Nearly 3,000 people turned up, crowding the house and grounds and lining the streets. Though many had come from sheer curiosity, he felt gratified. Hundreds were invited inside the mansion to feast and drink his health. He planned to wait until they had raised their glasses, then make a grand entrance and thank them all. But he spoiled everything at the last moment. Furious that 'the gost' had not shed a tear at his passing, he rushed out and gave her a good hiding.

But his real funeral was not so far away. In the autumn of 1806, in his 59th year, he died after a brief illness. His great house became first a hotel, then a library. A terrible storm destroyed most of his painted wooden statues (the rest that could not be sold, including that of Dexter himself, were put on a bonfire). Only the great golden eagle on the roof survived: and, fortunately, a few copies of his 'littel book'.

Dog's dinner

His pets were waited on by servants

Nothing but the best was good enough for his dogs, declared Francis Henry Egerton, eighth Earl of Bridgewater. That, to everyone's astonishment, included providing them with the finest and softest leather boots for all four feet.

These boots cost him as much as his own, but the man who made them was only too happy to oblige. Egerton had a passion for footwear which he could well afford to indulge. He himself wore a new pair of boots or shoes every day of the year. The hundreds of pairs he had discarded were arranged

Francis Henry Egerton

in orderly rows around the walls of his house and used as a calendar to count the days of the year.

A lonely man, who seldom invited anyone to visit him or to dine, he seemed to prefer canine company. He often took half a dozen or more dogs riding with him in his carriage and every day he dined with his four-footed friends. He would have the table set for 12 people, then his favourite dogs were brought in with napkins tied round their necks. Dressed in the height of fashion for these extraordinary meals, with servants behind their chairs to attend to every want, they were expected to eat from plates while he conversed with them. The Earl said his dogs behaved themselves as well as any gentleman – 'with decency and decorum'. If one of them happened to behave literally like a dog, it was banished from the table until it had learned better manners.

Only one other thing mattered to him – books. Egerton, whose immense fortune enabled him to satisfy every whim, was a considerable scholar, a patron of the arts and a Fellow of the Royal Society. If he borrowed a book, it was returned in style. He would order his finest carriage, place the volume inside and send four footmen in magnificent livery to escort it to its rightful and astounded owner.

He lived in Paris for some time and became a familiar figure about the streets in his huge 'sugar loaf' hat which was always pulled low over his eyes. The French treated him with good humour but did not approve of his practice of keeping pigeons and partridges with clipped wings in his garden so that he could still take a pot shot at them in spite of his failing eyesight.

The Earl of Bridgewater never married and with his death in 1829 the title became extinct, but his name lives on because he donated an important collection – the Egerton manuscripts – to the British Museum.

Riches to rags

She made millions and didn't give away a cent

Every morning when the Seaboard National Bank in New York opened its front doors, a grim-faced woman wearing ancient, rusty black clothes, ten years out of fashion, stalked in and seated herself behind a desk in the foyer.

She greeted no one but was soon immersed in wheeling and dealing, apparently conducting her business from a pile of cheap trunks and suitcases strewn around the floor.

Nobody got too near her. She stank. But everyone treated her with respect, even awe. For one thing, she had a foul temper. For another, she happened to be Mrs Hetty Green, one of the richest women in the world – and one of the meanest.

So mean was Hetty that she would spend half the night looking for a lost two-cent postage stamp; she wouldn't pay rent for an office and she rode around in a carriage that had once been considered too derelict for anything but a henhouse. Yet at the turn of the century her annual income was seven million dollars, and she even managed to evade the three per cent tax that was due!

She was born Hetty Howland Robinson on November 21, 1835, and came from a long line of Quakers with money-making in the blood. The building of their immense fortune started when a Howland ancestor bought 'one black cow' in Plymouth, Massachusetts, in 1624. From then on through generations of farming, land sales, slave trafficking and whaling, the millions piled up.

Her father, Edward Mott Robinson, was a tough, ruthless Philadelphian who had married for money and looked forward to setting up his own dynasty. He was appalled when his wife announced she could have no more children and he realized his only heir was a bad-tempered little girl.

But little Hetty soon won him over. By the age of six she was reading the financial pages in the daily papers. She would sit on his knee and listen to him quote from the stock market report. Her aggressiveness and understanding of money made him feel he had a son after all.

When he died he left her a fortune worth six million dollars in liquid assets. That would have been more than enough for most women, but not Hetty. She learned that her Aunt Sylvia, a Howland, had made a will distributing her two million dollar fortune to charity. She wanted that as well and fully intended to get it. Her plotting and scheming was the talk of the decade, but she failed after contesting the will with an apparently forged document.

To everyone's astonishment, Hetty became a bride at the age of 33. She was by no means an unattractive woman in her prime, having a fine figure, peach-coloured complexion and ice-blue eyes. Her husband, Edward Henry Green, member of a wealthy Vermont family, fell in love with her at first sight. Perhaps love blinded him – he seemed to have made no protest when his adored one made him renounce all rights to her fortune before the wedding!

For a time they lived in the bridegroom's splendid Manhattan apartment, but when news reached Hetty that her Howland cousins were seeking ways to bring her to court for forgery in connection with another of her interminable financial battles, she showed fright for the first time in her life and, with Edward, fled to London.

For the next eight years they lived at the exclusive Langham Hotel, where her two children, Ned and Sylvia, were born. Hetty didn't mind. She wasn't footing the bills.

On their return to America she soon tired of domesticity and being a wife. She quarrelled about every penny with her in-laws, her husband and her servants. Every shopkeeper in the neighbourhood detested her. Her only real interest was increasing her investments. She couldn't even be bothered to wash, and the hands that dealt in millions of dollars were usually dirty with black-rimmed nails.

When her marriage ended after 14 years and Edward Green decided to retire to the peace of his club, Hetty moved into a shabby furnished apartment in a seedy part of Brooklyn with her two unfortunate children in tow. She never turned on the heat even in the coldest weather and insisted there was nothing wrong with cold water for washing and bathing, if you went in for that sort of thing.

Most of the time she wore an ancient black dress which had turned a queer shade of green over underclothes that were never changed until they fell to pieces. Her shabby handbag was always stuffed with cheap broken biscuits bought from a corner store so that she need never buy a meal in a restaurant.

Her meanness even extended to her children – though she was genuinely fond of them – and they were dominated by her till the day she died. Her son Ned never had proper medical attention for a deformed leg and ended up with a cork one. It didn't stop him having a colourful public career and a somewhat lurid private life. Away from his mother, he lived lavishly, ran up enormous bills and sometimes hadn't a cent in his pocket. Her daughter Sylvia was a pathetic, drab young woman who wore outmoded clothes and couldn't dance because she had hammer toes. Hetty discouraged all Sylvia's suitors, saying they were only after the family fortune. When she did finally give her consent it was only after her future son-in-law had promised to waive all rights to her property and money!

Once her children had left 'home', Hetty decided her apartment was too spacious for her requirements. She moved to two shabby furnished rooms on the fifth floor of an apartment house. She would have preferred to make do with one, but much of her business was done in the evening when brokers and prospective borrowers called – she was primarily a money-lender with foresight that amounted to genius – and modesty prevented her from receiving them in a room with a bed in it.

Hetty Green, the richest and meanest woman in America

She insisted on handling everything herself and would journey thousands of miles to collect a forgotten debt of a few hundred dollars – always travelling in the cheapest possible way and taking her own food.

Restaurants were anathema to Hetty – unless someone else was paying the bill. When she worked at her desk in the bank she always brought her own lunch – not sandwiches like normal people, but a tin of oatmeal which she heated on the office radiators. She ate a huge bowl of it every day – bone dry. She said it gave her strength to fight 'the wolves of Wall Street'. And of course it only cost her a fraction of a cent.

As she grew older she became even more formidable. Her mouth set in a thin line and her jaw jutted with grim determination. But even Hetty's determination couldn't fend off ill health. She began to get discomfort from a particularly bad hernia – probably caused by hauling heavy account books from the bank vaults to her desk – and decided, whatever it cost her, to see a doctor.

When told she should have an operation, she demanded to know how much it would cost. The doctor, knowing her reputation, swallowed hard: 'My fee will be 150 dollars, hospital charges extra.' There was a moment's silence, then Hetty shrieked, 'You're all alike. A bunch of robbers.' Although the doctor had every right to be angry, he found the situation comical. When he asked for his 15-dollar examination fee he thought she would have apoplexy. 'She shuffled about under her coat for ages and eventually produced it from her handbag which was tied round her waist with string!'

As Hetty's fortune grew and grew she became obsessed with the idea that she was marked out to be kidnapped or robbed and went to great trouble to throw her would-be 'attackers' off the scent. She would take circuitous routes, double back on her tracks and even hide in doorways. She even began to think that her father and aunt had been poisoned by their enemies.

She died after a stroke when she was 80, leaving behind one of the greatest fortunes in the world. Nobody knew for sure *exactly* how much she was worth. Wall Street made a low estimate of 100 million dollars, though admitted it could be nearer 200 million. Within 40 years it had all been dispersed – and because she gave not a cent to charity, no hospital, college or library perpetuates her memory – only those stories of her incredible meanness.

CURIOUS CLERICS

Hiding behind a dog collar are some of the most
delightful crackpots of all. Clergymen usually have the
most gentle eccentricities – but you never quite know
what they will get up to. There was the parson who
couldn't stop dancing . . . and the archbishop who put
his feet into other people's pockets . . .

The odd Vicar of Morwenstow

He sat on the rocks singing like a mermaid

On the wild North Cornish coast, not far from Bude, there is a sheltered spot among the gorse-clad cliffs called Morwenstow. The grey tower of Morwenstow church stands silhouetted against the Atlantic. Cross an ancient stone stile and two fields dotted with sheep and you come to precipitous cliffs that drop straight into the sea. The place is incredibly beautiful. It is also haunted by the ghost of one of the most extraordinary vicars the Church of England has ever ordained.

Morwenstow was the parish for 40 years of the Rev. Robert Stephen Hawker, poet, rebel, hero of shipwrecked sailors and a character so colourful that he bursts through the pages of Cornish history like a rocket. He was a man of immense vigour and action. Smugglers and wreckers alike treated him with grudging respect. Yet he was also a man who would spend hours alone in a hut which clung precariously to the cliff face, watching the Atlantic in all its moods from glittering calm to raging storm, writing his poetry.

He was a big man in every way, broad, tall, with a handsome, mobile face and a thundering, rich voice. One of the few times he was seen in an orthodox black cassock was in the early days after his induction. He found he couldn't scramble around the cliffs in it or negotiate the slithery black rocks on the beach in shipwreck weather. He abandoned it for a claret-coloured coat, a bulky fisherman's jersey, long sea boots and a peculiar brimless hat.

Morwenstow had been without a resident vicar for a century before Hawker went there in 1835. He found he had taken on a parish full of villains, his manse was in ruins and the church was neglected and gently rotting amidst a forest of weeds and nettles. But he grew to love it.

Much of the ceremonial he used in the church was entirely his own and for some odd reason, he always wore scarlet gloves. Baptizing a baby, he would raise it in his arms, stride up and down the church in his flowing purple cape and roar out: 'We receive this child into the congregation of Christ's flock.' It was very dramatic and parents would travel miles for a Hawker baptism. At weddings he would take the ring and toss it into the air before allowing the bridegroom to have it.

He was usually followed to church by nine or ten of his pet cats which prowled around the chancel during the service. Originally there were ten but when one caught a mouse and ate it on a Sunday, he excommunicated it. While saying prayers he would absent-mindedly scratch his favourites under their chins. A little dog sat on the altar step with him in the position usually occupied by the server. Asked why he didn't turn it out he answered, 'All animals, clean and unclean, should find refuge here!'

His church was terribly untidy and full of strange bits and pieces he had collected which had nothing to do with religion. Above the screen was a large cross painted bright blue with five gold stars on it, representing the cross of the southern sky. Near the pulpit he kept a grotesque, garish piece of carving representing a castle attacked by a two-headed dragon. His chancel was strewn with wormwood, sweet marjoram and thyme; his altar was strewn with old burnt-out matchsticks and candle-ends. The church was furnished partly from his kitchen and he used a tumbledown old stable on the north side of the chancel as his vestry.

The untidiness offended one officious young curate. One day this man swept up all the rubbish he could find – old decorations left from past Christmases, musty dried roses, pages of old Bibles, prayer books and discarded poems – and piled it into a wheelbarrow. He then trundled it to the vicarage, rang the bell and asked for Hawker.

'This is the rubbish I have found in your church,' said the curate self-righteously. Hawker looked down at him and pursed his lips. 'Not at all,' said the vicar with deceptive mildness. 'Complete the pile by seating yourself on top and we'll see the whole lot speedily got rid of. . . .'

Robert Hawker came from a family of clergymen and was born on December 3, 1804. A well-to-do aunt sent him to Cheltenham Grammar School and from there, after earning a prize reputation for mischief, he went hopefully to Pembroke College, Oxford. Unfortunately, his father's stipend as a poor curate was not enough to keep him at Oxford. Robert decided to find a way. His method was somewhat drastic.

Hearing that a Miss Charlotte I'ans had inherited an annuity of £200 a year as well as lands and a handsome house, he tore off to propose to her. She accepted and they were married when he was 21. The fact that the lady happened to be his godmother, aged 41 and a year older than his mother did not deter him one bit.

On his vacations from Oxford he built himself a cliff top perch where he could be alone and write his poetry, a great deal of which is very fine and reflects his great love of Cornwall and Cornishmen. Most people remember him best for his 'Song of the Western Man', better known as 'Shall Trelawny die?'

But he also had a wicked sense of humour. One elaborate trick he played on the superstitious people of Bude is recounted by S. Baring Gould in his biography of Hawker. At full moon in July 1825, he rowed out to a rock some distance from shore where he plaited seaweed into a wig and threw it over his head so that it hung in lank streamers half-way down his back. He wrapped his legs in oilskin, but otherwise sat stark naked on the rock, flashing the moonbeams about from a hand mirror. He 'sang and screamed' until a crowd gathered. Word spread that a mermaid with a fish's tail was sitting on a rock, combing her hair and singing. A number of people ran out onto the rocks and along the beach and listened awestruck to the disconsolate wailing of the 'mermaid'. Presently, she dived off a rock and disappeared. This went on for several nights, the crowd growing bigger and more curious. At last, Hawker grew suspiciously hoarse and became tired of sitting on wet rocks in the nude. He wound up his performance one night with an unmistakable 'God Save the King', plunged into the waves and was never seen off the shores of Bude again.

He took Holy Orders and was ordained to a curacy in North Tamerton when he was 25. The parish had never had a curate like him before. He rode bareback on a rough pony, always accompanied by a black pig called Gyp. He was very fond of this pig – which was of the Berkshire breed – and it was cared for, washed and curry-combed till it shone. It ran beside him when he went for walks and even followed him into drawing rooms. If told to leave, it did so with great dignity, 'being an intelligent and obedient creature'.

At last, to his great joy, Hawker was offered the church at Morwenstow. He threw himself into the local life with zeal. There were shipwrecks galore on that treacherous coast and he was as daring as any man. No sooner had the call gone out that another ship was on the rocks than Hawker was on his way, striding out in his high seaman's boots, risking life and limb in the raging sea. Those he rescued from the water were taken back to his vicarage, nursed, fed, reclothed and sent away with gifts. Letters came from shipowners all over the world thanking him for what he had done for their men.

He came to have an intense sympathy for the wretchedly paid farm labourers in his parish and fought for them with vigour. On cold winter nights, when the wind tore in from the Atlantic, he would take bottles of brandy from his cellar, meat from his larder and blankets from his beds, and tour the poor cottages to see if anyone was in need.

He wore his own clothes until they were threadbare and had no best suit in which to receive visiting bishops. Sometimes on cold days he could be seen riding through the lanes on the back of a mule – the only fitting beast, he remarked, for a churchman – and wearing a yellow garment which made him

The Rev. Robert Stephen Hawker

look like a Tibetan lama. He took a great delight in explaining to the more gullible of his flock that it was an exact copy of the robes worn by ancient Cornish saints, who had a great affinity with the East. In fact, it was a yellow blanket bought in Bideford and made into a poncho by cutting a hole for the head!

The truth was that he hated anything black, and even when his first wife died he had to be persuaded to tie a piece of black ribbon round his strange, plum-coloured, brimless hat for the funeral. He was utterly bereft when Charlotte left him and moped about the cliffs for days on end. He got the idea that he could eat nothing but clotted cream, ate it for breakfast, tea and dinner and became extremely bilious.

People still flocked to the vicarage which he had built beside the church at Morwenstow. For one thing, he kept open house. The visitors also came to see his curious chimneys, which had been built as miniature replicas of his favourite church towers. But he was very lonely without a wife and eventually married again, this time a Miss Kuczynski, daughter of a Polish nobleman, who through reduced circumstances had become governess to a local clergyman.

Hawker's last days were not happy. He was harrassed with financial worry. His church was in a terrible state of repair. He did not know how he was going to provide for his wife and three children after his death. Worry and illness at last forced him to take a holiday. In 1875, at the suggestion of his wife, he travelled to Plymouth, to see a doctor and to rest. He walked out to the cliffs for a last look at the scene he loved so much, sensing that he would never see it again. Soon after, he died in Plymouth, and though he would never have wished it, was buried there.

For years after, people in Morwenstow said they had seen the great figure of Robert Hawker in the churchyard, wandering among the wind-blown graves where he should have lain with his first wife and his shipwrecked sailors.

The dancing curate

He wrote mystery novels and Drury Lane tragedies

When the Rev. Charles Robert Maturin took up dancing, he became an addict. So passionately fond was he of wearing out shoe leather that he never wanted the night to end. He would close the shutters of his house, even when the sun was shining, and light the

The Rev. Robert Maturin who was addicted to dancing

candles; then, behind darkened windows he would pretend the ball had just begun and dance until his feet were sore.

His zest was incredible. He wore out dozens of pairs of dancing shoes each season and none of his friends could keep up with him. When his wife, not unnaturally, began to complain, he hit on the idea of organizing morning quadrille parties at his friends' houses and two or three times a week pranced about on their carpets till they were threadbare.

Ever since he was a child in Dublin, Maturin had loved striding about in fancy dress and displaying his shapely legs and lively footwork in theatricals. He had a great sense of the dramatic, probably inherited from his family, which had a colourful history. He came from a line of French Huguenots, one of his ancestors having arrived in Ireland after spending 26 years in the Bastille.

Graduating from Trinity College, Dublin, in 1800, Maturin married young and chose the Church as a career. He soon found that a curate's stipend did not allow for his exotic tastes. Burdened with financial embarrassment, he began to write. Romantic novels with titles like *The Fatal Revenge* and *The Wild Irish Boy* poured from his pen. These were followed by a succession of lurid-Gothic novels and plays in which horror piled up on horror with monotonous regularity. They were an enormous success. He crossed the water to London, where he was greeted as a celebrity. Some of his tragedies were produced at Drury Lane with the great actor Kean in the leading roles. Kean, however, was not too happy with the parts Maturin wrote for him and, when offered yet another gruelling tragedy to read, tactfully lost it.

Still, the profits enabled Maturin to buy a house in York Street, Dublin, where he painted the ceiling with clouds and eagles and the walls with scenes from some of his novels.

He danced with glee, but not for long. He seemed to have no idea how to manage his life and constantly veered from wealth to poverty. Everyone knew from the way he dressed how life was treating him; his wardrobe changed from showy opulence to plain shabbiness, according to the state of his bank balance. However, he insisted that his wife, Henrietta, must always be beautifully groomed and rouged. Royalties would be used to dress her in what he considered the height of fashion, even if the larder was empty.

As the years went by, the Rev. Maturin became terribly absent-minded. He quite often turned up for parties a day late and sometimes paid social visits wearing a boot on one foot and a shoe on the other.

He drifted off into another world when he was writing his novels and pasted a wafer on his forehead as a sign to his family that he was not to be addressed. Guests invited for dinner at such a time often fared badly. He would forget they were there and let the food go cold on the table. One of his last books, *Melmoth the Wanderer*, turned out to be his masterpiece and still has its admirers, only recently being reprinted in America.

He was only 42 when he died in 1824. His end was hastened by absent-mindedly taking the wrong medicine.

The astonishing Archbishop

He couldn't keep his feet still

His Grace, the Protestant Archbishop of Dublin was in full flow after a splendid dinner, his conversation peppered with the puns for which he was famous. But, for once, his wit raised little more than a titter. All eyes were fixed with horror on his right foot.

He had raised it into the air, doubled it back over his left thigh, grasped the instep with both hands as though about to strangle it, then, with a final contortion, dumped it into the lap of Provost Lloyd sitting next to him. And there it stayed while Archbishop Whately recounted some very funny stories. It was said, to his credit, that the provost didn't turn a hair while his best black suit was treated like a doormat.

On another occasion, the archbishop was sitting next to Chief Justice Doherty at a Privy Council meeting in Dublin. Doherty, feeling a sneeze coming on, groped in his pocket for a handkerchief only to find Whately's foot already in there!

Richard Whately, Protestant primate of Dublin from 1831 to 1863, must have been one of the most restless men who ever lived. His brilliant mind worked at twice the rate of that of most people. Furthermore, his limbs were never still.

He was especially jumpy while waiting for meals. At Lord Anglesey's home in Ireland, where he was a regular guest, he would pull a chair up to the fire, stretch out his legs, then swing them onto the mantlepiece and rest them alongside some extremely rare pieces of Dresden china.

Lady Anglesey would only just manage to hold her tongue. Whately had already dislocated half a dozen of her most elegant chairs by whizzing them round and round on one leg while he talked, and there were patches of bare carpet in front of the fireplace where he would shuffle to and fro while warming his bottom. Sometimes, bored with waiting, and being totally disinterested in social chit-chat, he would take out a pair of scissors and trim his nails, or make miniature boomerangs out of his visiting cards and send them flying round the room.

In fact, so amiably eccentric was his behaviour that it was said that if people didn't know an anecdote about Richard Whately, they could always invent one. Many complained that he didn't behave like an archbishop – but

The Archbishop of Dublin, Richard Whatley

perhaps that was because he never expected to become one and would much rather have lived a comfortable rural life, teaching and preaching and pruning his trees.

Born into a family littered with clerics – his father was the Rev. Joseph

Whately of Bristol – on February 1, 1787, he was chiefly noted during his boyhood for being appallingly absent-minded. He concentrated only on what interested him. He would spend hours in the garden watching the habits of spiders, but never kept up with local births, deaths and marriages, and was wholly ignorant of the names of the streets and shops in the neighbourhood.

When he was 18 he entered Oriel College, Oxford, and after taking his degrees stayed on to become one of the most controversial dons of his generation. The Oxford he knew was extremely orthodox and conservative. Whately was liberal-minded, a progressive thinker, and blunt with it. He was always being misunderstood because he was so outspoken and failed to cultivate the social graces.

When he preached, however, he drew enormous crowds. For one thing, people wanted to see what he would *do*. It was generally known that he had no sense of proper clerical dignity. Once during a sermon he 'worked his leg about to such an extent that it glided over the edge of the pulpit and hung there till he had finished'. The congregation was helpless with laughter.

He lectured his pupils lying flat on a sofa with his legs dangling over the arm. Sometimes they were invited to accompany him on long walks with his three dogs. This usually involved climbing a few trees. Whately would clamber up into the branches and leave a handkerchief or pocket knife for his hounds to sniff out – a sort of canine treasure hunt.

When he left Oxford for a spell to take up the living of Halesworth in Suffolk, one wag said that the university felt it had got rid of a nightmare and could settle down to sleep again. But after four years of rural bliss he was called back to become principal of St Alban's Hall. The more pious prayed that he had become a more decorous don. They soon found that life as a country parson had not changed him one bit. A commentator in *The Times* summed up the situation perfectly: 'The university goes one way and Richard Whately the other.'

It would be difficult to say who was the more surprised when he was offered the Archbishopric of Dublin – Whately or his colleagues at Oxford. Nobody had thought for a moment that he was a likely candidate for the mitre. He had no connections with Ireland, no ambitions for wealth and power. He never courted favour and was perfectly happy as he was, living with a delightful wife and occasionally shocking the Oxford dons.

But Lord Grey, the Prime Minister, had chosen him for other obvious qualities and he knew he must accept as a matter of duty. He always considered he'd made a sacrifice. He just hoped that once his character was understood, the Irish might appreciate him better than his former colleagues.

His optimism did not last long. Dublin was resentful of the government's policy of appointing Englishmen to positions of power in Ireland and he was met with suspicion and mistrust. Consecrated archbishop on October 23, 1831, he felt at first like an alien in his own church.

Irish mistrust soon turned to confusion. They didn't know what to make of an archbishop who sat on the chain fence outside his Palace smoking a long clay pipe and who could be seen whirling round and round his garden with a boomerang, clambering up trees and playing hide-and-seek with his dogs!

Whately looked like a farmer or a seaman with his fresh, ruddy complexion and shock of unruly hair. He had succeeded Archbishop Magee, who was something of a dandy and trotted out on horseback each morning to be admired by the faithful. Whately, by contrast, hated the pomp and ceremonial that went with being an archbishop. In his memoirs of Whately, written in the last century, William John Fitzpatrick says the Order of St Patrick, when he was obliged to wear it, hung round his neck as a thing that was in his way and which he would gladly have dropped into the nearest wastepaper basket. He was always forgetting or losing it. Once when he appeared at William IV's court without the medal, he was ordered to send home for it.

His tastes were extremely simple. When he moved into the Palace on St Stephen's Green, Dublin, he loathed the ornate gilded decorations that had cost his predecessor a fortune and threatened to have them all whitewashed. He lived frugally – but some people felt economy was taken too far when he used worn-out church vestments for gardening.

He found the Protestant church in Ireland in terrible disorder, the clergy lax and discipline poor, and he set out to reform it. This made him enemies. But he was tough and outspoken. He once asked a clergyman who had spoken out against him: 'Pray, sir, why are you like the bell of your own church steeple?' 'Because,' answered the cleric cleverly, 'I am always ready to sound the alarm when the church is in danger.' 'By no means,' retorted the archbishop. 'It is because you have an empty head and a long tongue.'

Whately got on well with the Catholics and had an amiable relationship with the dignified Roman Catholic primate, Archbishop Murray. One of his greatest achievements was the way in which he won the cooperation of Murray and the bulk of the Catholic hierarchy in establishing the great scheme of national education in Ireland.

They would meet for discussions, together with distinguished men like the Duke of Leinster and Lord Plunket, round a large conference table. Sometimes Whately rested his feet on it. Usually he threw his chair backwards, making it rest on its two back legs, then he would start to swing. He wore a hole in the carpet which was for years pointed out as 'Whately's hole' until the carpet had to be replaced.

He had taken up phrenology, the science of reading character from the shape of the head, and when he got bored at these meetings he would try to sum up the virtues and failings of those present.

'Have you heard of the latest phrenological test, gentlemen?' he asked one day. 'Take a handful of peas, and drop them on the head in question. The amount of the man's dishonesty will depend on the number that remain there. If a large number stay put, tell the butler to lock up the plate!' Unfortunately he said all this without taking his eyes from the singularly flat skull of a highly respectable provost.

Children loved him. They would smile and greet him cheerfully as he walked with his dogs on St Stephen's Green. He argued that children should be free to enjoy any pastime they liked on the Lord's Day. He was totally against gloomy Sundays, and the Calvinists in his congregation thought his ideas worthy of the devil.

But when it came to kindness and generosity, no one could fault him. He gave away most of his personal fortune. His acts of charity were carried out quietly and without show. During the terrible years of the potato famine he instructed his clergy to help anyone in need, regardless of whether they were Protestant or Catholic.

Sometimes he made people to whom he lent money sign a document, swearing that when they had enough they would repay the debt – not to himself but to anyone else they could find in desperate need.

His family life was extremely happy. He loved his garden and would walk round it twice a day with a heavy walking stick which had a steel blade at one end. As he walked, he lashed out at weeds and lopped and pruned without interrupting his step. He believed an outdoor life could cure anything. If he had a headache he would go out in his shirt-sleeves, whatever the temperature, take an axe and hack away at the toughest tree trunk he could find. When the tree had been felled and he was dripping with perspiration he would get into bed, wrap himself in a blanket and fall sound asleep. When he woke he was usually full of beans and the headache gone.

He was devoted to his wife. When she died in 1860 after 38 years of marriage, he sat on the stairs and wept like a child. Indeed, from then on his robust health began to fail. Doctors despaired of him. He would take no drugs or medicines and told them to throw them out of the window. He was disabled by a final stroke and eventually died in great pain, though surrounded by friends.

People in Dublin suddenly realized how much they were going to miss him. They would never again see him taking the air on St Stephen's Green, working his arms round and round like a windmill, throwing pebbles at the crows and romping with his dogs. Archbishops like Richard Whately do not come along very often.

TRAVELLERS' TALES

Crackpots have spread their eccentricities across the earth. Throughout history, travellers extraordinary have given the world something to talk about . . . like the playboy who went about in an iron wig . . . and the spinster who spent her life chasing butterflies and men . . .

Eastern adventurer

Married to a washerwoman, he posed as an Ottoman Prince

Edward Wortley Montagu bought himself an iron wig in Paris in the summer of 1750. It caused a sensation in London. 'You literally would not know it from hair,' wrote Horace Walpole in a gossipy letter to a friend. The wig was worn rakishly with a different satin suit and a different set of diamonds every day, adding no end to his already dazzling reputation.

But the sensation was nothing compared to the time some years later when, having embraced Islam, he turned up in a saffron turban with a jewelled, feathered 'aigrette', which only a true Prince of the Ottoman Empire was entitled to wear.

The famous traveller explained, to the fury of his mother, Lady Mary Wortley Montagu, that his headgear was suitable because he was not really his father's son, but the outcome of a passionate love affair between her and the Sultan of Turkey. He also said, without batting an eyelid, that while living in Constantinople she entered the 'seraglio', the Sultan's Holy of Holies, by posing as a eunuch!

For Lady Mary, herself somewhat eccentric, Edward's flight of fancy was the last straw. This beauty, wit and writer of some of the most eloquently entertaining letters in the English language, could only retaliate by calling him 'that animal' and, when she died, cutting him off with the proverbial shilling.

Throughout his life, Edward broke all the rules. He had a mistress at 13, as many wives as he fancied and almost as many religions.

He was born in 1713. His father, no Eastern potentate, was Edward Wortley Montagu senior, a studious English diplomat who, in spite of his enormous wealth, was a renowned miser. He eloped with the beautiful Lady Mary and neglected her shamefully ever after.

Edward was a weakly child and his mother wrote to her sister: 'I hope and beg of God that he may live to be a comfort to us both . . .' Little did she know what was to come.

When he was only three his father was made ambassador to Constantinople and the family moved out to Turkey. Smallpox raged through the

East and Lady Mary took what was then considered to be the wickedly eccentric precaution of having her infant vaccinated with the smallpox virus. He always said the inoculation changed his life, put Turkish blood in his veins and gave him a passion for far-off places.

Returning home two years later, Edward proved too precocious for all his tutors. He swore at them fluently in Greek, Turkish and French and would not do his lessons. His parents packed him off to Westminster. He hated it. The restrictions of an English public school were beyond bearing for a boy of his spirit. He ran away time after time, only to be found, beaten and sent back. Once he changed his clothes with a young sweep to earn a living brushing chimneys. Another time he apprenticed himself to a poor fisherman and was caught selling flounder from a basket in London's Rotherhithe.

At 13 he ran away to Oxford, enrolled himself as a student of Oriental languages, and lodged wth a buxom young landlady who became his mistress.

His mother wrote to a friend: 'That young rake, my son, took to his heels t'other day and transported his person to Oxford, being, in his own opinion, thoroughly qualified for the university. After a good deal of search we found and reduced him, much against his will, to the humble condition of a schoolboy.' She added wistfully: 'It happens very luckily that the sobriety and discretion are on my daughter's side. I am sorry the ugliness is too, for my son grows extremely handsome ...'

Poor woman, within four months he was gone again, this time for two years. 'I am vexed to the blood by my young rogue of a son who has contrived at his age to make himself the talk of the whole nation,' she groaned. 'He has gone knight erranting, God knows where, and 'tis impossible to find him ...'

Edward was on board a merchant ship bound for Portugal. He had again changed clothes with a boy his own age and begged the captain to take him as a cabin boy. When he landed in Oporto he took to his heels and the hills. He worked as a mule driver and was perfectly happy living a simple, free life until one day, delivering goods to the port, he was recognized by the British consul and returned to his despairing parents. Foolishly trying to keep their wild colt on a tight rein, the Montagus sent their son off to the West Indies with a tutor; but at the age of 17 he returned to London to sow his wild oats with a vengeance. One night, in a fit of high spirits, he married a young washerwoman called Sally. It was the silliest thing he ever did. He had to maintain her for the rest of his days.

After this escapade he was packed off to a dull backwater in Holland with the inevitable tutor and a stingy allowance of £300 a year. He kept himself sane by studying Arabic and, in a series of comically contrite letters, begged to be allowed home, to go into a monastery or even to marry a wealthy girl of his father's choice – he had already forgotten that he was a husband. But it was four years before he was set free.

He joined the army in Flanders, served as an officer at the Battle of Fontenoy and impressed everyone but his mother by his highly coloured account of his part in the action. In fact, the nearest he came to danger was being blown off his horse. Taken prisoner by the French, he was forcibly kept quiet for a spell.

After his release, a different Edward began to emerge. He became a considerable scholar in oriental languages, sat as a Member of Parliament for Huntingdon, acted as secretary to Lord Sandwich at the signing of the Treaty of Aix-la-Chapelle and was made a Fellow of the Royal Society.

But he was still an incorrigible rogue. By 1750 he was flaunting himself round London again and astonishing the world by his extravagance – and his debts. Horace Walpole, whose letters give a vivid picture of 18th-century life, informed a friend: 'Our greatest miracle is Lady Mary Wortley's son. His expense is incredible. His father scarce allows him anything yet he plays, dresses, diamonds himself and has more snuff boxes than would suffice a Chinese idol with a hundred noses. But the most curious part of his dress, which he brought from Paris, is an iron wig; you literally would not know it from hair ...'

One day Edward went to commiserate with the fashionable highwayman, James McClean, who had recently been caught and clapped behind bars. Women were fascinated by McClean and two beauties were in his cell when he arrived. One of them was a tiny, pert blonde called Elizabeth Ashe. Edward fell in love with her, married bigamously and ran off to Paris for their 'honeymoon', gleaming with diamonds and wearing his iron wig.

When his millionaire father eventually died, Edward was in for a shock. He had left the bulk of his fortune not to his gadfly son, but to his quiet, smug daughter, Mary, who was married to the Earl of Bute.

Edward was horrified and humiliated. Despite an annuity of £1,000, to be raised to £2,000 on his mother's death, he was not the heir. Elizabeth Ashe lost interest and allowed herself to be drawn back into the social whirl.

His ego sorely bruised, he decided to turn his back on the world of glitter and frivolity and become a scholar. He intensified his study of Arabic and immersed himself in books about the East, and set out on a great journey that was to last for 10 years. He discarded his iron wig in favour of a turban and grew a long beard.

In 1763 he sailed for Egypt. His first port of call was Alexandria where he scooped up the Danish consul's wife, Caroline Feroe, while her husband was away on business and 'eloped' with her down the Nile.

Edward Wortley Montagu

The beautiful Caroline was the daughter of an Irish father and an Italian mother, bored by her upright Protestant husband and delighted to be wooed by this electrifying Englishman with his impeccable manners and flashing dark eyes. She readily fell for Edward's fabricated story that Herr Feroe had been drowned at sea and she trailed after her lover through the villages on the banks of the Nile, trying to learn Arabic while he absorbed himself in astronomy and hieroglyphics.

They went through a form of marriage at Rosetta but on hearing that Herr Feroe had returned to Alexandria and was about to set off in pursuit, Edward whisked the bemused Caroline off to the Sinai peninsula. 'Like Moses pursued by Pharaoh's host,' he wrote afterwards, 'I guided my steps towards the wilderness.'

It was an odd honeymoon. Edward wandered through Sinai with an Old Testament in one hand and the Danish consul's wife in the other. He followed the path of the Exodus, stood on the very rock where Moses came face to face with God, and discovered the gap in the mountains through which the Israelites passed on their way to the Red Sea. The travel papers he sent home were read admiringly at meetings of the Royal Society.

But Caroline began to grow fretful. Edward seemed to spend all his time studying ancient graffiti under an unbearably hot sun and had little time or energy left to play the ardent lover. She reminded him it was time he kept his promise to turn Catholic and have her marriage to Herr Feroe declared null and void.

Turning away from the wilderness, Edward tried to get his affairs in order. He took Caroline to Jerusalem, was received into 'the bosom of the Holy Church', then left her in a convent while he carried on to Venice where he hoped to expedite the documents that would free her from the Dane.

He was amazed by his reception in Venice. As he had just returned from the plague-ridden Orient, he had to go into quarantine and was accommodated in quarters that were separated from the rest of humanity by a corridor. But practically every Englishman in Venice came to see him and listened with rapt attention as he talked of his travels.

His beard now reached to his waist in a cascade of perfumed braids and ringlets. He wore a colourful Armenian headdress and flowing robes, slept on the ground, drank only water and allowed himself no luxuries other than tobacco and coffee.

Away from Caroline, matrimony seemed less attractive and he spent the next few years roaming. He was said to be the first Englishman ever to enter Constantinople bearded, turbaned and speaking fluent Turkish.

Eventually he returned to Egypt where the patient Caroline managed to pin him down and they were remarried in a Roman Catholic ceremony. They set up home together at Rosetta but Edward had his own ideas on how it should be run. Despite his conversion, he proclaimed that he intended to live the rest of his life as an Arab and divided his house into the 'selamlik' (men's quarters) and the 'haremlik' (women's quarters).

Only two things disturbed him. The presence of his Irish father-in-law and the allure of a black Egyptian serving-girl called Ayesha. In the end he gave his father-in-law an ultimatum to leave. He no longer bothered to conceal his passion for the luscious Nubian either – and the storm broke. Caroline departed with her troublesome father, leaving Ayesha to console her husband.

Edward had no doubt been consoled by Ayesha on many previous occasions. She had a child, a handsome black boy called Massoud who was now brought up as Edward's own son. He embraced the Moslem faith and went through a marriage ceremony with the black girl. To please her, he took to wearing round his neck a phallic amulet, in the form of a pair of dried goat's testicles!

He decided to crown his achievements by making the pilgrimage to Mecca. There was only one obstacle. He had never been circumcized. By now he was 60 and, everyone insisted, far too old. He retorted that Abraham had been 99 when he had submitted to the knife and nobody had objected to that operation.

But he was never to make the journey to Mecca and his marriage to Ayesha was no more durable than the rest. Growing restless, he took Massoud back to Europe and settled in Venice. In his Venice palazzo, he entertained sitting cross-legged on cushions, Turkish fashion, and served his guests Turkish coffee in small white cups like eggshells resting on gold pedestals, while his young negro slave, magnificently dressed in aquamarine satin, handed them dried figs and rahat lokum.

He saw no one till noon. The morning was devoted to putting his luxuriant beard in curling papers, proudly boasting that it was an outward sign of his faith in the Prophet.

He was attended by two huge black eunuchs wearing nothing but silver bracelets, ankle rings and small 'modesty nets' of metallic mesh. His gondola flew a Turkish royal pennant, and his head was swathed in the saffron coloured turban that had maddened his mother. He was always preceded by two gondoliers holding tall, lighted torches, even on the sunniest days, and pageboys held his white robes out of the dust.

Suddenly his idyll was disrupted by a startling piece of news. He heard that Sally, the washerwoman he had married so light-heartedly all those years ago, had died.

His father's will had empowered him to make a settlement of £800 a year on any woman he might marry *legally*, and any legitimate son would be entitled to a considerable estate in Yorkshire. He felt it was not too late to get himself a proper wife.

Naturally, he went about it in the most bizarre way. He advertised for a widow or single lady of gentle birth and polished manners who was six, seven or eight months pregnant. If suitable, he would marry her and the estate would pass on in his name.

Fate was to deprive him of any such satisfaction. Several women answered his advertisement, but their letters arrived too late.

One night his favourite dish was served for supper – grilled ortolans, tiny succulent birds, cooked Italian fashion on a skewer. A sharp wing bone stuck in his throat and despite all their efforts, the doctors could not dislodge it. An abcess formed, infection spread and soon he could eat nothing but yoghourt.

As he lay dying, his bedroom was crowded with friends. when a priest asked him in what faith he would leave the world he answered firmly: 'I hope – a good Musselman.' He passed into a coma and died early in the morning of April 29, 1776.

He never knew that the 'legal' marriage on which he set such store could never have taken place. The friend who told him of Sally's death had been misinformed. The washerwoman outlived him.

The original Phileas Fogg

George Train went round the world four times

One fine July morning in 1870, wealthy American businessman George Frances Train set out on one of the most famous journeys ever made. He went Around the World in Eighty Days. Two years after his return he found himself immortalized in Jules Verne's famous story. Verne had changed him into Phileas Fogg, the peripatetic Englishman. But the source was obvious. Train was not at all pleased. 'He stole my thunder,' he protested. '*I'm* Phileas Fogg.'

George Train, who managed to cram three or four lifetimes into one by doing everything at incredible speed, preferred to blow his own trumpet. Fogg was presented in Verne's book as a clipped, precise Englishman, a pillar of the Reform Club. But Train was an erratic, unconventional Bostonian, one of the founders of the Union Pacific Railway. Fogg was a cool, unemotional man. Train was impulsive and explosive. Fogg made the journey for a wager in the best British sportsmanlike manner. Train did it because he was bored, and, being a whirlwind of a man, couldn't stay in one place for more than five minutes.

Both men had at least two things in common, however: they both loved storms and typhoons and they both spent money like water when it came to chartering transport.

George Train's journey around the world was an extraordinary feat in an era of sailing ships, buggies and erratic 'iron horses'. He set out from New York, travelling through Red Indian country to reach San Francisco by the shortest possible route. From there he sailed for the Orient, arriving in Japan 25 days later (astounding the Japanese by leaping into a public bath in the nude). On he went to Hong Kong, Saigon and Singapore, through the newly opened Suez Canal and from there to Marseilles.

His reputation as something of a rebel and a supporter of 'causes' had already reached France. When he landed, the locals begged him to forget his journey and become leader of their 'commune'. He declined, but couldn't resist dabbling in politics, and missed his next train. At Lyons, he was mistaken for a Red revolutionary and thrown into jail. It was only through the intervention of his friend, Alexandre Dumas, the US President himself, the *New York Sun* and the London *Times* that he was eventually bailed out and expelled. Having lost a precious 13 days, he hired a private train and raced across France to the Channel. Once in England, he headed straight for Liverpool, caught a boat by the skin of his teeth and arrived in New York 80 days after setting out (excluding the forced stop in Lyons).

George Train, a dark, handsome man propelled by what he called his 'psychic forces', was 41 when he first circled the globe. He was to do the trip again three more times, finally, at the age of 63, completing the circuit in a mere 60 days.

The first journey of his restless life was made at the age of four. It was a traumatic experience. The Train family was living in New Orleans when a yellow fever epidemic hit the town. It struck like a plague and people were dying so fast they had to make their own coffins. Young George lost his mother, father and three sisters. It was decided to send him to safety with his maternal grandparents in Massachusetts. He travelled alone on a cargo boat, with an identity card pinned to his coat, and was 23 days at sea without a change of clothing and with very little to eat.

Having survived such a journey, George Train obviously felt he was to make his mark on the world. His strict Methodist grandparents wanted him to be a clergyman when he grew up. But as he turned out to be an atheist, they had to let him work in a grocer's shop instead. His job was hard and uninspiring. One day his father's wealthy cousin, Colonel Enoch Train, came visiting in a fine carriage and George was deeply impressed. *That*, he decided, was his life style.

He found out where Colonel Train's shipping office was in Boston and next day turned up on the doorstep. 'Where do I come in?' he asked. His audacity paid off. Within two years he was manager of the firm and within four years, a junior partner earning $10,000 per annum.

Speed was the secret of his success. He was always interested in finding out how fast things could be done. He got rid of the Colonel's ageing clippers and talked him into buying bigger, faster ships. But when business boomed and he asked for a full partnership as a reward, the Colonel almost had apoplexy. George decided it was time for him to see the world.

Off he went to Melbourne, Australia, and joined with gusto in the Gold Rush. Dissatisfied with rough buildings thrown up by the 'Aussies', he had a six-storey warehouse shipped out to him from Boston, built his own offices in the main street and set out to make a fortune. He sold gold, offered transport services faster than anybody else, and imported the sort of goods Australians had never seen. George was fascinated by 'Down Under', but it was not the world – and he wanted to see the world. After two years he was off through the great cities of the Far East, India, Palestine and Egypt. The *New York Herald* published 16 columns of his letters from abroad and he was asked to run for Congress.

Back home he soon showed that he was a man to be reckoned with. One day he was dining at a hotel in Omaha. He took objection to the manager's behaviour and considered he had been slighted. Within a few hours he had purchased an empty lot across the street, sketched a crude plan of a new and better hotel on the back of an envelope and offered a contractor $1,000 a day if he would complete the building in 60 days. Train went off on holiday and returned to find the three-storey, 120-room Cozzens Hotel standing ready to take its first guests!

By now he had acquired a wife and daughter and, in spite of his devotion to revolutionary causes, a snobbish desire to mingle with European aristocrats. In 1856 he arrived in Paris, took a suite at a luxury hotel and proceeded to mingle, later boasting that he had actually talked in French to the Empress Eugénie.

He went on from Paris to Rome, where he was again received with revolutionary fervour and nearly mistaken for Garibaldi, and from there to

Russia, where he found Moscow to be the most impressive city he had ever seen.

Somehow he always managed to get mixed up with liberation armies and revolutionaries, though, in fact, he loathed violence and was terrified of guns. During his lifetime he managed to frequent 15 jails, and at one point five or six governments kept their spies shadowing him in Europe and America.

On all his journeys he became involved in financial deals. His last major venture was the financing and building of the Union Pacific Railway in America. Vanderbilt told him: 'If you attempt to build a railway across the desert and over the Rocky Mountains, the world will call you a lunatic. . . .' He went ahead. Before he was 40 he was a millionaire and admitted he had done too much, too easily and too quickly.

What was left? He couldn't bear to be out of the limelight, so he went into politics. He became convinced that he was the greatest man in the world and due to be President, but, in fact, people described him as 'a messiah without a message' and 'a half-baked thinker, half genius and half fool'.

He became sole candidate for the Citizens' Party and, resplendent in a blue swallow-tailed coat with brass buttons, stomped up and down the country delivering 1,000 speeches. He could hardly have expected to win. In the middle of his campaign he took off on the journey that transformed him into Phileas Fogg.

He had an alarming tendency to land in prison. After publishing a column of quotations from the Bible relating to sexual intercourse in order to prove some point or other, he was arrested on obscenity charges and clapped in Tombs Jail. While there he gave interviews to the press, dressed in a fashionable sealskin coat, and became bosom friends with a murderer known as 'the famous Sharkey'. Sharkey was so impressed with George that he had him elected President of Murderers' Row.

Everyone knew that the obscenity charge was weak and that they had trouble on their hands as long as George was behind bars. Police were instructed to leave his cell door open, make deals with him, invite him to leave – anything. But he refused to take any notice and insisted upon a trial, whereupon the judge, knowing he was hooked, tried to bring in a verdict of 'guilty but insane'. George was furious and after that began to call himself 'The Great American Crank', playing the part with huge enjoyment.

He became a vegetarian and believed if he ate enough peanuts he would live to be 150. Instead of shaking hands with other people he shook hands with himself, the manner of greeting he had seen in China. For a time he also refused to talk to anyone and wrote messages on a pad when he wanted to communicate. These were means, he explained, of storing up his psychic forces. He even invented a new calendar, based on the date of his birth.

Gradually he lost all his money and had to support himself by writing and lecturing. With his long white hair and flowing moustache, he was a marvellous sight on any platform. He usually wore a military coat with a scarlet sash and a string of Chinese coins hung round his neck; and he also carried a bright green umbrella.

He lived in a tiny room furnished with a bed, a chair and a pile of crates stuffed with his papers. In this room he wrote articles for a weekly he published under the name *Train's Penny Magazine*, in which he railed against religion, mail-order houses and the Spanish-American War. He also dictated his biography, admitting in it: 'I have lived fast. I have ever been an advocate of speed. I was born into a slow world and I wished to oil the wheels so that the machine would spin faster....'

He spent his last days on a bench in Madison Square Gardens, feeding the squirrels and playing with the children. He was 75 years old when he died on January 4, 1904, in New York City. Hundreds of people who remembered his most resplendent days went to see him lying in state.

The great animal tamer

Friend of apes and crocs who opened the world's first game park

The great 19th-century English naturalist Charles Waterton once captured a crocodile by jumping onto its back, seizing its front legs in a judo hold and riding it like a cowboy on a bucking bronco. Asked how on earth he had managed to keep his seat, he replied modestly that he had hunted for some years with Lord Darlington's foxhounds.

Waterton seemed to fear nothing he encountered in the wild territories of the world. He walked through jungles barefoot, and his bravery made him a legend.

In Guiana he set out to capture a live boa constrictor so that he could examine its teeth. Native guides helped him to grab an ideal victim but were terrified by the huge, thrashing snake. Waterton urged them to hold on to it until it could be manoeuvred into a sack, but their courage gave out. Just as they were about to drop it and run, Waterton whipped off his braces and bound the snake's jaws.

Vampire bats fascinated him. On one of his expeditions to South America he caught one and shut it into his room at night. He then climbed into his hammock and slept with one foot dangling over the side, hoping that the bat would be attracted by his big toe. He wanted to be bitten so that he could record the effects of the creature's toxic poison. But the bat ignored Waterton's toe and zoomed down on an unfortunate Indian who shared his quarters. Waterton never tried the experiment again.

His reputation as a naturalist was established by four journeys he made to South America and the jungles of Brazil, the first in 1812. Though unorthodox, he was recognized as one of the foremost experts on birds and animals in that part of the world and a book he wrote about his travels became a best-seller.

When he eventually settled down in England, it was to succeed his father as squire of Walton Hall, the family home in Yorkshire.

His appearance set him apart from other Englishmen. He was tall, lean and bronzed with a clean-shaven chin and close-cropped hair at a time when most men's faces were buried in whiskers and when hair was luxuriant.

He also had great charm, kindness and unsuppressible gaiety.

When he moved into Walton Hall he baffled neighbours by building an eight-foot fence around three miles of his estate. Behind it he created a garden which became the first bird sanctuary and wildlife park in the world.

Friends would sometimes call only to find he had shinned up one of the immense oak trees and was perched in the topmost branches, watching the birds coming and going and building their nests.

Visitors would find strange animals wandering freely around the house. Waterton loved all living things – except for brown rats, which he detested – and had a special fondness for nature's quirks. He owned a small albino hedgehog with pink eyes, and a duck which had no webbing between its toes. His closest companion for a time was a Brazilian toad. He was extremely angry when a visitor called it an 'ugly brute'. A three-toed sloth lived for months in his room, where it would hang from the back of a chair.

His favourite hobby was taxidermy and he assembled an enormous collection of stuffed animals. He created extraordinary monsters by joining parts of two or three different corpses together. These were distributed all over the house and visitors were often frightened out of their wits when they stumbled across one of Waterton's creations in a dark passage. An ardent Catholic, he delighted in naming his more grotesque specimens after famous Protestants.

All his life, Waterton insisted that he was the most commonplace of men and that it would be impossible for him to do an eccentric thing. Yet he once dissected a gorilla on his dining-room table after the remains of the meal had been cleared away.

A great practical joker, he would sometimes enter a room on all-fours or even walk on his hands with his feet in the air, laughing uproariously when he saw the surprised faces around him. He would hide in the hallway and, pretending to be a dog, nip his friends in the shins as they left their hats and coats on the hall table.

His agility was remarkable. He was still scrambling up trees at the age of 80, looking, remarked writer Norman Douglas, 'just like an adolescent gorilla'.

As a young man, he once climbed to the top of the angel which surmounts the Castel San Angelo in Rome and entertained the crowds below by standing on one foot on the angel's head. He also clambered up the lightning conductor on the roof of St Peter's and left his gloves as a visiting card. The Pope was furious – but as nobody else could be found with the nerve to retrieve them, the devout Waterton made a return journey.

Waterton had a unique relationship with animals. One of the most striking proofs was his meeting with an enormous orang-utan at London Zoo.

The orang-utan had just been shipped from Borneo and was proving extremely savage. Waterton asked if he could see it and, gazing at it through the bars, was struck by the sadness in its eyes. The curator tried hard to discourage Waterton when he asked permission to go into the cage. A small crowd gathered and watched fearfully as he and the orang-utan came face to face.

The onlookers were astounded to see Waterton and the orang-utan throw their arms around each other and hug with delight. The great ape allowed Waterton to inspect its teeth and the palms of its hands, and returned the compliment by plunging its fingers into Waterton's mouth and appearing to count his molars. The two then sat together and the naturalist submitted to a thorough grooming. They parted with obvious regret and the encounter was the talk of the zoological world.

Waterton once examined a cheetah's claws with the same success, quietly entering its cage and using his strange talent to smooth its aggression.

His life at Walton Hall was deeply affected by the death of his young wife in 1830. From that day he would not sleep in a bed. Instead, he wrapped himself in a cloak and lay on the floor with a block of beechwood for a pillow. He would rise at 3.30 a.m., light his fire and, after an hour in his private chapel, start his day's work. His breakfast always consisted of dry toast, watercress and a cup of watery tea without milk.

Charles Waterton, the great English naturalist

Though best known for his love of animals and birds, he was unfailingly kind towards fellow human beings. He regularly threw open the grounds of the hall so that cotton workers could have a day in the fresh air, and twice a year he entertained patients from the local mental hospital, dancing with them on the lawns and rowing them on the lake.

No one in the neighbourhood was allowed to go barefoot. They could always rely on getting a new pair of boots from the squire. Once he met a tramp whose feet were bleeding. Waterton promptly gave him his own shoes and walked home in his socks.

His jacket pocket was always bulging with stale bread so that he could feed any hungry bird or squirrel he might meet on his walks.

Waterton, who died in 1865, had aroused consternation and admiration for many of his 83 years. When he died he was buried between two great oaks in the park – and local legend has it that flights of birds followed his coffin to its resting place.

Charles Waterton

Butterflies and beaux

She debated with entomologists and hobnobbed with bandits

Miss Margaret Fountaine was a fascinating English spinster who spent all her life falling in love and chasing butterflies. Wearing a pair of plimsolls and a rather large cork sun helmet, she climbed mountains, tramped through jungles, slept in flea-ridden huts from Damascus to Tibet in the hope of snaring prize specimens for her collection, and while trekking through some of the world's most dangerous territory armed with nothing more lethal than a butterfly net, she managed to capture both lepidoptera and men!

She was one of that bumper crop of determined and eccentric lady travellers produced by the vicarages of Victorian England, but the full story of her intrepid travels and equally intrepid love affairs only came to light many years after.

Her magnificent collection of 22,000 butterflies, mounted in ten great mahogany cases, was bequeathed to the Castle Museum, Norwich, in 1940, on condition that the curator also accepted a sealed black metal box, which was not to be opened until April 15, 1978.

No one had the faintest idea what was inside, but when the seals were broken it was found to contain 12 volumes of her diaries – 3,000 pages of vivid prose written in a neat, sloping hand, along with photographs, drawings, postcards and pressed flowers. (Some were edited and published in book form by W. F. Cater, an assistant editor of the *Sunday Times*, who had already fallen under her spell.)

Existing photographs of this rather prim, doleful-looking lady convey no idea of the passionate creature she undoubtedly was – especially when wearing her butterfly-hunting costume. This consisted of a man's check shirt with several extra canvas pockets sewn on, a striped cotton skirt with more pockets, cotton gloves with the fingertips cut off, the large cork helmet and the inevitable plimsolls. Her chest was festooned with various bits of equipment including a heavy black chain with a compass on one end.

She spent so long in the sunny places of the world that she dreaded going home to England. But whenever she did return, she would shop for clothes. She bought half-a-dozen pairs of plimsolls at a time, and was especially fond of the top people's London store, Harrods. Once, when going out to India, she decided to buy some dresses as she had been invited to stay with the Viceroy. She chose silk ones, perfectly suitable for Viceregal garden parties. The dressmaker was horrified when Miss Fountaine told her to slit open the side seams and insert two large canvas pockets. 'They'll hang alright for the party,' she explained. 'Then I'll fill them with butterfly boxes afterwards.' She saw nothing in the least peculiar about wearing a Harrods dress with plimsolls for scrambling round in the dust after butterflies.

For a time she had a studio in Hampstead as her base camp in England. It was starkly simple. She would stay just long enough to deal with her affairs then suddenly decide to go on another expedition. Up she would jump from the breakfast table, throw a few things into a bag and set off for the other end of the world, leaving the remains of her meal on the table. Her accountant, obviously an understanding man, would go in and clear up, knowing that she might not be back for years.

Margaret Fountaine was the eldest daughter of a Norfolk country clergyman, the Rev. John Fountaine, rector of South Acre, a hamlet 20 miles from Norwich. She was born in 1862 and grew up, with seven brothers and sisters, in a world dominated by maids, governesses and nannies.

In her teens she went to church regularly and just as regularly fell in love with the curates. But it was her passionate infatuation for an Irish chorister called Septimus Hewson that really changed her life. Septimus was a cad and a drunk, though she would never admit it. She fell in love with him as he sang in Norwich Cathedral choir, pursued him round the cloisters in a most unladylike fashion and even wrote letters begging him to take pity on her. Septimus gave in for a time and they were almost engaged, but then he abandoned her for drink and another woman.

To mend her broken heart, Miss Fountaine decided to travel. Her uncle had just left her a modest income of £100 a year – enough, she reckoned, to enable her to see the world. With her sister as companion, she set out for Switzerland, then on to the hills of Tuscany, the Italian Lakes and Rome, all the time chasing butterflies and being chased by men. She was, by all accounts, far more attractive than the stiff Victorian portraits convey, and a typical entry in her diary reads: 'I spent most of my time with the Baron ... as I might have expected, he too ended by making me an improper proposition.'

Butterfly chasing had started as a pastime but quickly became an all-consuming passion. It was not in her nature to do things by halves. She cycled hundreds of miles through Italy, often to some straggling dirty village full of goats and chickens, spending hours scrambling over rocks and tangled undergrowth in pursuit of some elusive beauty. It was really an extraordinary feat when one remembers the appalling roads of those days, not to mention the cumbersome ankle-length skirts.

From Italy, on to Corsica where in the rugged mountains she met up with bandits, including the infamous Jacques Bellacoscia, a Corsican hero who had started his career by shooting the mayor of Ajaccio. 'I drank with Jacques,' she wrote, 'and sometimes in the quieter walks of life, I love to look back upon that wild mountain scene, the outlaw and his clan, the savage dogs who prowled about among the grey rocks and the purple heather . . .' So impressed was she by Jacques that she kept a piece of Corsican heather in her diary.

She remained on the island for a while, in pursuit of butterflies which she knew existed nowhere else. As for men, her method of dealing with tough-looking customers likely to have guns hidden under their velvet jackets was to swear at them for all she was worth. However, on one expedition 'a wild, gypsy looking fellow' insisted on carrying her equipment. 'So intense was my keenness in pursuit of entomology that I felt no fear whatever to wander out into the country quite alone with this man,' she wrote naively. In the end she escaped from his clutches by leaping over a ditch in her plimsolls.

Nothing could stop her now. In Hungary she was greeted with open arms by the Budapest entomologists (and a little too warmly by a certain Dr Popovitch). She accompanied them on their annual outing into the mountains, went on an expedition with a certain tall, fair Herr Torok for whom she felt a rising passion, and would sometimes trek for nearly 12 hours with nothing more than two pieces of bread and a mug of sheep's milk to sustain her. Inhabitants of the small Hungarian villages thought she was a harmless lunatic!

But it was in Damascus that Miss Fountaine was to meet the love of her life. She was 39 when she engaged a 24-year-old Syrian courier called Khalil Neimy to escort her through the Middle East. He was fair for an Arab, wore his tarboosh jauntily on the back of his head and spoke in a strong American accent. He fell madly in love with her at first sight, offered to be her servant for nothing more than his keep, and smothered her hands and arms with passionate kisses. The Norfolk parson's daughter bristled with indignation at first, and then succumbed.

She discovered later that he already had a wife and two children, but his story was a sad one and she forgave him. He was her devoted lover and companion for 28 years, until his death, and she insisted that her magnificent collection of butterflies should be named the Fountaine-Neimy Collection so that his name would be remembered.

Together they travelled through some of the wildest places in the world, frequently where no white woman had been seen before. Conditions were often appalling: 'I passed a terrible night on the floor – the place was infested with fleas and vermin,' she wrote after staying in some filthy little village in order to capture a beautiful white butterfly.

After a particularly bad dose of malaria in North Africa she started to bathe in diluted creosote to deter leeches and other pests. It turned her to a darker shade of brown.

Still highly susceptible to men, she admitted that on a trip to Crete she was 'consoled' by the flattering though highly improper suggestions of an Egyptian ship's officer. Travelling to the tropics, where butterfly after butterfly was popped into specially made, white, ant-resistant boxes, she found the African bush frightening but a proposal of marriage by a Frenchman flattering. Poor Khalil once had to pretend he was her brother to preserve the status quo.

Eventually an ecstatic Miss Fountaine reached Sikkim, the butterfly collector's paradise, and, hiring a sturdy Tibetan pony, rode over hair-raising precipitous paths through the 'cloud land of the Himalayas, a world of wild winds and bitter cold and strange, curious faces'. Her childhood dreams were realized as she stood looking down into Tibet, but she was only to have a glimpse of that mysterious country. A huge, unmelted mass of snow and ice blocked the Chumbi Valley and they had to turn back.

She never stopped travelling. There are stories of her being lost in the African jungle, caught in an earthquake in Cuba, chasing exotic specimens in Fiji. When she visited her relations in America she earned money by collecting spiders' nests at four dollars a dozen and accepting orders for butterflies off the Californian hills. She surprised her young nephew by playing a skilled game of pool. Her energy was prodigious. When she was nearly 70 she rode 45 miles a day on a butterfly expedition, most of it at the gallop.

But she was most incorrigible when it came to mixing love and butterflies. On one journey, when she set out to explore the regions along the great rivers of South America, she was pursued relentlessly by an amorous Brazilian. At a crucial point in their relationship, the Norfolk parson's daughter wrote: 'It forced itself upon my unsuspecting brain that very soon he would be *out* of his pyjamas ... it reminded me of the days of long ago.'

Her travels ended on a dusty road in Trinidad one day in 1940. She had collapsed in the heat and when a kindly monk, Brother Bruno, found her, she was already dying of a heart attack. Her beloved butterfly net lay just out of reach beside her.